-knitted-
with
love

24 Simple and Easy to Knit
Patterns for Babies & Children

By Jane Ellison

Wool, the love you can feel.

I am so passionate about knitting and natural fibres, especially wool. I think this passion is in my blood. My mother researched our family history and there is one long branch that is linked to Yorkshire and the woollen mills as far back as the records go. Every single person in this line worked in the mills, with job descriptions varying from 'mill girl' to 'mill owner'. My grandfather was a wool buyer (who married into this line as he worked for his wife-to-be's father) and my great grandfather was a woollen mill owner who learnt his trade as an apprentice at Salts Mills, Saltaire.

I grew up in the south of England (in a town called Bradford on Avon, which also has a very strong wool heritage as it grew in the 17th Century due to the thriving English woollens textile industry) unaware of this branch of my family as I set about casting on my first knit stitch as a seven year old, knitting a scarf (in 100% wool of course) for my Snoopy toy.

One symptom of my love of wool is that I get excited about different breeds of sheep and their wool qualities. Not all sheep produce the same sort of wool – far from it!

The qualities are amazing – did you know for example that wool can help you regulate your body temperature? A 100% wool jumper or cardigan will keep you cool in summer and warm in winter, they insulate you like a vacuum flask. This seems hard to believe in our world of readily available synthetic fibres that make you too hot and overheat, or don't keep you warm enough but try wearing one and you'll see for yourself!

That's why beautifully soft wool is perfect for babies and children who are learning to regulate their body temperature. Wool offers invaluable assistance as it is naturally breathable, making baby more comfortable and, in turn, that means those looking after baby are happier too!

Wool is totally unique, just like your little one, and nothing else compares to it. With every calming stitch you are taking time to look after yourself and the garment you create will help look after your little one.

Hello

Welcome to my book of simple and easy to knit patterns for babies and children. Working on this book has been an absolute joy for me and I hope you love knitting these patterns as much as I have loved designing them. Please share pictures of your finished items with me – one of my favourite things about being a hand knit designer is seeing the unique spins that different knitters put on my designs.

There are 16 garments, three hats, four blankets and one pair of socks all designed in varying sizes from newborns to 10 year olds depending on the style of the garment.

Nothing says I love you like a hand knit item knitted with that special little someone in mind. It's perfect for wrapping up children of all ages with warmth, comfort and happiness.

When designing for this book I had lots of different knitters in mind. The first group is knitting rookies who want to make something beautiful and full of love for the new little one in their life – whether it's their own new baby or a niece, nephew, grandson, granddaughter or great granddaughter or great grandson!

Then there's those returning to knitting, who haven't knitted for a while and just need a simple, easy to knit pattern to ease them back in slowly.

Lastly there are knitters like me who always need knitting; simple, easy knitting to pick up at the end of a busy day or to relax with on rainy days. For me there is nothing like relaxing in a favourite chair with the rain gently falling against the windows while you curl up with your favourite hot drink, calm and relaxed while knitting little items to give as gifts of love and joy.

I believe that knitting is as much about the journey you go on when creating the item – the joy of the rhythmic motion of beautifully soft yarns moving through your fingers and the calm that comes with making one stitch after another – as the unique finished items you make. So enjoy the process as much as your little ones will enjoy their new, special gift.

Happy Knitting,

Hubberholme
ON PAGE
32

By Jane Ellison

Birbeck
ON PAGE
34

By Jane Ellison

Bell Beck
ON PAGE
36

By Jane Ellison

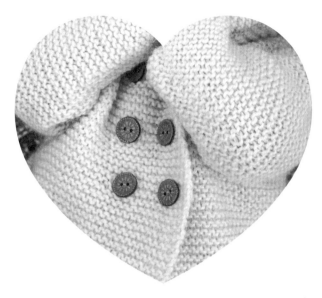

Hazle
ON PAGE
52

By Jane Ellison

Lenny
ON PAGE
40

By Jane Ellison

**Ghyllas Cardigan
& Sepperdin Blanket**
ON PAGES
CARDIGAN 42
& BLANKET 69

Strid
ON PAGE
48

By Jane Ellison

Strawberry Bank
ON PAGE
46

By Jane Ellison

Crag
ON PAGE
56

By Jane Ellison

Cherry Tree
ON PAGE
50

By Jane Ellison

Oxenber Tank Top
& Calton Gill Blanket
ON PAGES
TANK TOP 72
& BLANKET 39

Danny Brow
ON PAGE
62

By Jane Ellison

Sun Moor
ON PAGE
28

By Jane Ellison

Gamsber
ON PAGE
64

By Jane Ellison

Bell Beck Jumper
& Clapdale Hat
ON PAGES
JUMPER 36
& HAT 49

By Jane Ellison

Rukin
ON PAGE
77

By Jane Ellison

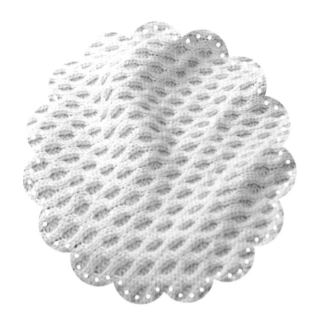

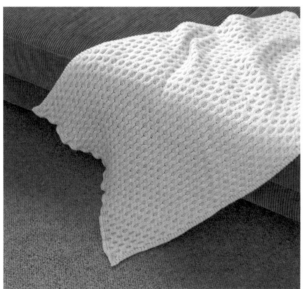

Hawking Pots
ON PAGE
67

By Jane Ellison

Brockabank Jumper & Hanlith Hat
ON PAGES
JUMPER 60
& HAT 66

By Jane Ellison

**Brockabank Jumper
& Wharfe Hat**
ON PAGES
JUMPER 60
& HAT 75

By Jane Ellison

Raydale
ON PAGE
54

By Jane Ellison

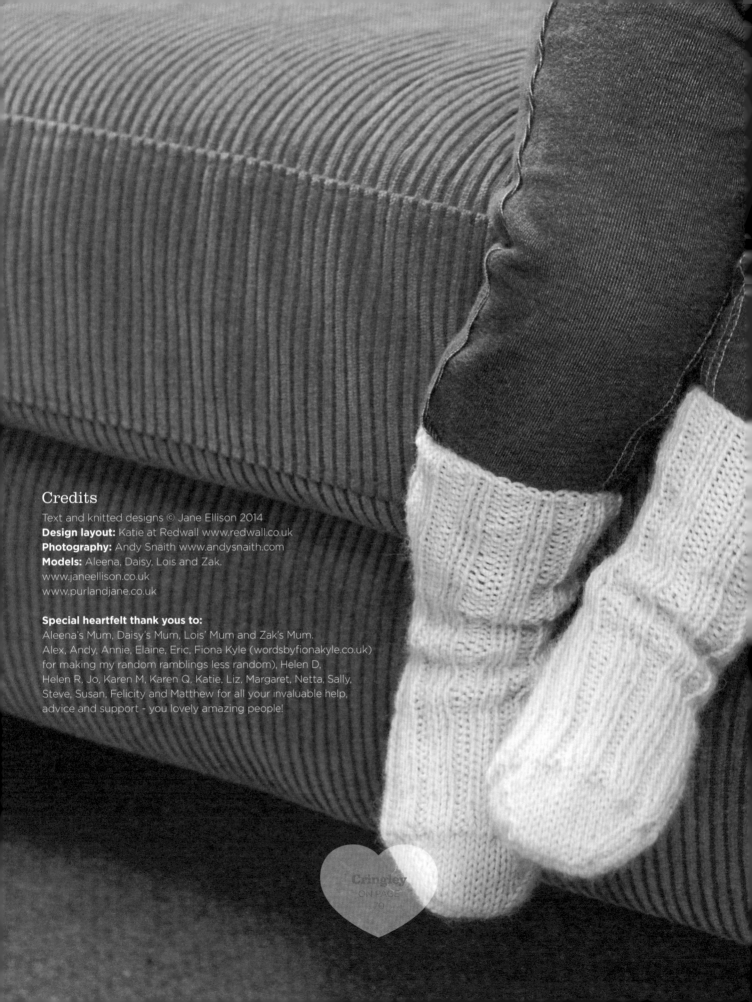

Credits

Text and knitted designs © Jane Ellison 2014
Design layout: Katie at Redwall www.redwall.co.uk
Photography: Andy Snaith www.andysnaith.com
Models: Aleena, Daisy, Lois and Zak.
www.janeellison.co.uk
www.purlandjane.co.uk

Special heartfelt thank yous to:
Aleena's Mum, Daisy's Mum, Lois' Mum and Zak's Mum.
Alex, Andy, Annie, Elaine, Eric, Fiona Kyle (wordsbyfionakyle.co.uk)
for making my random ramblings less random), Helen D,
Helen R, Jo, Karen M, Karen Q, Katie, Liz, Margaret, Netta, Sally,
Steve, Susan, Felicity and Matthew for all your invaluable help,
advice and support - you lovely amazing people!

Cringley
ON PAGE
76

-knitted-
with
love

Patterns

Sun Moor

Matinee Jacket

MATERIALS

3(4:4:5:5) 100g hanks of aran weight yarn.
(this amount is based on aran weight
yarn with 166m per 100g)
Pair of 4.5mm knitting needles.
Pair of 5mm knitting needles.
4 buttons.

TENSION

19 stitches and 28 rows to 10cm/4ins square
over rib pattern using 5mm needles.
24 stitches and 32 rows to 10cm/4ins square
over cable pattern using 5mm needles.

MEASUREMENTS

to fit (suggested age)	1-2	3-4	5-6	7-8	9-10	yrs
actual chest measurement	**62**	**68**	**75**	**81**	**88**	**cm**
	24½	26¾	29½	31¾	34½	ins
length	**32**	**36**	**40**	**44**	**48**	**cm**
	12½	14¼	15¾	17½	18¾	ins
sleeve length	**20**	**24**	**28**	**34**	**40**	**cm**
	7¾	9½	11	13¼	15¾	ins

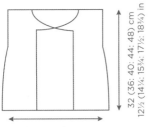

31 (34: 37.5: 40.5: 44) cm
12¼ (13¼: 14¾: 16: 17½) in

14 (17.5: 20: 20: 24) cm
5½ (6¾: 7¾: 7¾: 9½) in

32 (36: 40: 44: 48) cm
12½ (14¼: 15¾: 17½: 18¾) in

20 (24: 28: 34: 40) cm
7¾ (9½: 11: 13¼: 15¾) in

This jacket is inspired by traditional matinee jackets and I have used my favourite cable pattern. I love how the only two stitches you need to make a pattern are knit and purl and that they can be used in different positions to create beautiful effects.

So simple yet so stunning.

I love the garter stitch mixed with the plain stocking stitch in the rib and then with the cable, to me it looks like the ridges of the garter stitch are joining the cables together.

back

With 5mm needles, cast on 65(72:79:86:93) stitches.
Knit 2 rows.
1st rib row (right side): knit to end.
2nd rib row: k2, [p5, k2]to end.
These 2 rows form the rib pattern.
Repeat the last 2 rows until back measures 22(24:26:28:30)cm/8¾(9½:10¼:11:11¾)ins from cast on edge, ending with a wrong side row.
Increase row (right side): k2, [k4, m1, k3]to end.
74(82:90:98:106) stitches
Next row: k2, [p6, k2]to end.
1st row (right side): [k4, C4F]to last 2 stitches, k2.
2nd and every alternate row: k2, [p6, k2]to end.
3rd row: k2, [C4B, k4]to end.
These 4 rows form the cable pattern.
Repeat the last 4 rows until back measures 32(36:40:44:48)cm/12½(14¼:15¾:17½:18¾)ins from cast on edge, ending with a wrong side row.

shape shoulders
Cast off 20(23:26:28:30) stitches at the beginning of the next two rows.
Leave centre 34(36:38:42:46) stitches on a holder.

left front

With 5mm needles, cast on 47(54:62:69:77) stitches.
Knit 2 rows.
Next row (right side): knit to end.
Next row: k2, [p6, k2]3(3:4:4:5) times, *p5, k2, repeat from * to end.
1st row (right side): knit to last 24(24:32:32:40) stitches, [k2, C4F, k2]to end.

2nd and every alternate row: k2, [p6, k2]3(3:4:4:5) times, *p5, k2, repeat from * to end.
3rd row: knit to last 24(24:32:32:40) stitches, [C4B, k4]to end.
These 4 rows form the pattern.
Repeat the last 4 rows until left front measures 22(24:26:28:30)cm/8¾(9½:10¼:11:11¾)ins from cast on edge, ending with a **2nd row.**
Increase row (right side): k2, [k4, m1, k3]3(4:4:5:5) times, [C4B, k4]to end. 50(58:66:74:82) stitches
Next row: k2, [p6, k2]to end.
1st row (right side): [k4, C4F]to last 2 stitches, k2.
2nd and every alternate row: k2, [p6, k2]to end.
3rd row: k2, [C4B, k4]to end.
These 4 rows form the cable pattern.
Repeat the last 4 rows until left front measures 26(30:34:36:40)cm/10¼(11¾:13¼:14¼:15¾)ins from cast on edge, ending with a **right side** row.

shape left neck
Next row (wrong side): pattern 26(30:34:38:44) stitches, leave these stitches on a holder, pattern to end. 24(28:32:36:38) stitches
Decrease row: pattern to last 3 stitches, k2tog, k1.
23(27:31:35:37) stitches
Work one row.
Decrease one stitch at neck edge on the next and every following alternate row until there are 20(23:26:28:30) stitches.
Continue without shaping in cable pattern until left front measures 32(36:40:44:48)cm/12½(14¼:15¾:17½:18¾)ins from cast on edge, ending with a wrong side row.
Cast off.

Sun Moor

right front

With 5mm needles, cast on 47(54:62:69:77) stitches.
Knit 2 rows.
Next row (right side): knit to end.
Next row: k2, [p5, k2]3(4:4:5:5) times, *p6, k2, repeat from *
to end.
1st row (right side): [k2, C4F, k2]3(3:4:4:5) times, knit to end.
2nd and every alternate row: k2, [p5, k2]3(4:4:5:5) times, *p6, k2,
repeat from * to end.
3rd row: k2, [C4B, k4]3(3:4:4:5) times, knit to end.
These 4 rows form the pattern.
Repeat the last 4 rows until right front measures
22(24:26:28:30)cm/8¾(9½:10¼:11:11¾)ins from cast on edge,
ending with a **2nd row.**
Increase row (right side): pattern to last 21(28:28:35:35) stitches,
[k4, m1, k3]to end. 50(58:66:74:82) stitches
Buttonhole row (wrong side): k2, [p6, k2]to last 24(24:32:32:32)
stitches, p2, yon, p2tog, p2, k2, [p6, k2]1(1:2:2:2) time(s), p2, yon,
p2tog, p2, k2.
1st row (right side): k2, [k2, C4F, k2]to end.
2nd and every alternate row: k2, [p6, k2]to end.
3rd row: k2, [C4B, k4]to end.
These 4 rows form the cable pattern.
Repeat the last 4 rows until right front measures 25(28:32:34:38)cm/
9¾(11:12½:13¼:14¾)ins from cast on edge, ending with a **right side** row.
Work **Buttonhole row** once again.
Continue in cable pattern until right front measures
26(30:34:36:40)cm/10¼(11¾:13¼:14¼:15¾)ins from cast on edge,
ending with a wrong side row.

shape right neck

Next row (right side): pattern 26(30:34:38:44) stitches, leave
these stitches on a holder, pattern to end. 24(28:32:36:38) stitches
Decrease row: k1, s1, k1, psso, pattern to end.
23(27:31:35:37) stitches
Pattern one row.
Decrease one stitch at neck edge on the next and every following
alternate row until there are 20(23:26:28:30) stitches.
Continue without shaping in cable pattern until right front
measures 32(36:40:44:48)cm/12½(14¼:15¾:17½:18¾)ins from cast
on edge, ending with a wrong side row.
Cast off.

sleeves

With 5mm needles, cast on 26(32:38:38:44) stitches.
Knit 2 rows.

1st rib row (right side): knit to end.
2nd rib row: k2, [p4, k2]to end.
These 2 rows form the rib pattern.
Work the last 2 rows once more.
Increase row (right side): k2, [k1, m1, k2, m1, k3]to end.
34(42:50:50:58) stitches
Next row: k2, [p6, k2]to end.
Starting with a **1st row** of cable pattern as given for the back and
keeping pattern correct, increase one stitch at each end on next
and every following 4th row until there are 52(60:68:68:76) stitches.
Continue without shaping in cable pattern until sleeve measures
20(24:28:34:40)cm/7¾(9½:11:13¼:15¾)ins from cast on edge,
ending with a wrong side row.
Cast off.

edging

Join shoulder seams. With right side facing and 4.5mm needles,
work across the 26(30:34:38:44) stitches from holder at right
front as follows: k2, [s1, k1, psso, k2, k2tog, k2]to last 0(4:0:4:2)
stitches, [s1, k1, psso, k0(2:0:2:0)]0(1:0:1:1) time, to make
20(23:26:29:33) stitches, pick up and knit 11(11:11:15:15) stitches up
right front neck, work across the 34(36:38:42:46) stitches from
holder at centre neck as follows: k2(3:0:0:0), k2(2:2:0:2)tog, k2,
[s1, k1, psso, k2, k2tog, k2]to last 4(5:2:0:2) stitches, [s1, k1, psso,
k2(3:0:0:0)]1(1:1:0:1) time, to make 26(28:28:32:34) stitches, pick
up and knit 11(11:11:15:15) stitches down left front neck, work across
the 26(30:34:38:44) stitches from holder at left front as follows:
[k0(2:0:2:0), k2tog]0(1:0:1:1) time, k2, [s1, k1, psso, k2, k2tog, k2]to
end, to make 20(23:26:29:33) stitches. 88(96:102:120:130) stitches
Next row: k57(62:65:76:82), turn.

shaping shawl collar

1st row: k26(28:28:32:34), turn.
2nd row: k28(30:30:34:36), turn.
3rd row: k30(32:32:36:38), turn.
4th row: k32(34:36:38:40), turn.
Continue to work in this way, working 2 more stitches on each row
until all stitches are worked.
Cast off.

to make up

Sew on sleeves, placing centre of sleeves to shoulder seams.
Join side and sleeve seams. Position and sew buttons into place.

Hubberholme Jumper

Jumper with Turtleneck

This design was inspired by another childhood memory of fisherman's clothes – this time more modern smocks. With these shapes in mind, I played around with stitch details that were simple to knit but created an attractive effect.

MATERIALS

2(3:3:4:4) 100g hanks of dk weight yarn.
(this amount is based on dk weight
yarn with 225m per 100g)
Pair of 3.75mm knitting needles.
Pair of 4mm knitting needles.
One button.

TENSION

22 stitches and 30 rows to 10cm/4ins square
over narrow rib pattern using 4mm needles.

32 (36: 40: 44: 48) cm
12½ (14¼: 15¾: 17½: 18¾) in

29.5 (32: 35: 37.5: 40) cm
11½ (12½: 13¾: 14¾: 15¾) in

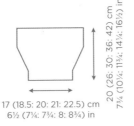

20 (26: 30: 36: 42) cm
7¾ (10¼: 11¾: 14¼: 16½) in

17 (18.5: 20: 21: 22.5) cm
6½ (7¼: 7¾: 8: 8¾) in

MEASUREMENTS

to fit (suggested age)	1-2	3-4	5-6	7-8	9-10	yrs
actual chest measurement	59	64	70	75	80	cm
	23¼	25¼	27½	29½	31½	ins
length	32	36	40	44	48	cm
	12½	14¼	15¾	17½	18¾	ins
sleeve length	20	26	30	36	42	cm
	7¾	10¼	11¾	14¼	16½	ins

By Jane Ellison

back

With 4mm needles, cast on 65(71:77:83:89) stitches.
1st rib row (right side): knit to end.
2nd rib row: p2, k1, [p5, k1]to last 2 stitches, p2.
These 2 rows form the wide rib pattern.
Repeat the last 2 rows until back measures 20(22:24:26:28)cm/
7¾(8¾:9½:10¼:11)ins from cast on edge, ending with a wrong
side row.
1st row (right side): knit to end.
2nd row: p2, [k1, p2]to end.
These 2 rows form the narrow rib pattern.
Repeat the last 2 rows until back measures 32(36:40:44:48)cm/
12½(14¼:15¾:17½:18¾)ins from cast on edge, ending with a wrong
side row.

shape shoulders

Cast off 17(17:20:20:23) stitches at the beginning of the next
two rows.
Leave the centre 31(37:37:43:43) stitches on a holder.

pocket lining (make two)

With 4mm needles, cast on 19(19:25:25:25) stitches.
1st row: knit to end.
2nd row: k1, [p5, k1]to end.
These 2 rows form the wide rib pattern.
Repeat the last 2 rows until pocket lining measures 10(10:12:12:14)cm/
4(4:4¾:4¾:5½)ins from cast on edge, ending with a wrong
side row.
Leave stitches on a holder.

front

Work as given for the back until front measures 10(10:12:12:14)cm/
4(4:4¾:4¾:5½)ins from cast on edge, ending with a wrong
side row.
Pocket placement row: work 8(8:8:8:14) stitches, cast off the next
19(19:25:25:25) stitches purlwise, work 19(19:25:25:25) stitches
along one pocket lining, work 11(17:11:17:11) stitches, cast off the
next 19(19:25:25:25) stitches purlwise, work 19(19:25:25:25) stitches
along remaining pocket lining, work to end.
Continue as given for the back until front measures
28(30:34:38:42)cm/7¾(8¾:9½:10¼:11)ins from cast on edge,
ending with a wrong side row.

shape left neck

Next row (right side): pattern 20(20:23:23:26) stitches, turn
and slip remaining 45(51:54:60:63) stitches onto a holder.
20(20:23:23:26) stitches
Work one row.
Decrease row (right side): pattern to last 3 stitches, k2tog, k1.
19(19:22:22:25) stitches
Next row: p2, pattern to end.
These 2 rows set the position of the decrease.
Decrease one stitch as set above at neck edge on
the next and every following alternate row until there are
17(17:20:20:23) stitches.

Continue without shaping in narrow rib pattern until front
measures 32(36:40:44:48)cm/12½(14¼:15¾:17½:18¾)ins from
cast on edge, ending with a wrong side row.
Cast off.

shape right neck

With right side facing, leave centre 25(31:31:37:37) stitches
on a holder, rejoin yarn to remaining 20(20:23:23:26) stitches,
pattern to end.
Work as given for shape left neck, working neck decrease
as follows:
Decrease row (right side): k1, s1, k1, psso, pattern to end.

sleeves

With 4mm needles, cast on 38(41:44:47:50) stitches.
Starting with a **1st row** as given for the back, work in narrow
rib pattern until sleeve measures 6cm/2¼ins from cast on edge,
ending with a wrong side row.
Keeping pattern correct, increase one stitch at each end on
next and every following 4th row until there are
54(57:62:67:68) stitches.
Continue without shaping in narrow rib pattern until sleeve
measures 20(26:30:36:42)cm/7¾(10¼:11¾:14¼:16½)ins from
cast on edge, ending with a wrong side row.
Cast off.

collar

Join right shoulder seam. With right side facing and 3.75mm
needles, cast on 2 stitches, pick up and knit 9(12:12:12:12) stitches
down left front neck, pattern 25(31:31:37:37) stitches from holder
at centre front, pick up and knit 8(11:11:11:11) stitches up right front
neck, pattern 31(37:37:43:43) stitches from holder at centre back.
75(93:93:105:105) stitches
1st row (wrong side): k1, [p2, k1]to last 2 stitches, k2.
2nd row: knit to end.
Repeat the last 2 rows until collar measures 2cm/¾in, ending with
a wrong side row.
Buttonhole row: k1, yon, k2tog, knit to end.
Work 2 rows.
Cast off.

to make up

Join left shoulder seam. Sew on sleeves, placing centre of sleeves
to shoulder seams. Join side and sleeve seams. Sew pocket linings
into place on the inside. Slip stitch buttonhole side of collar on top
of the other side of collar. Position and sew button into place.

Birbeck Jumper
Wavy Cable Jumper

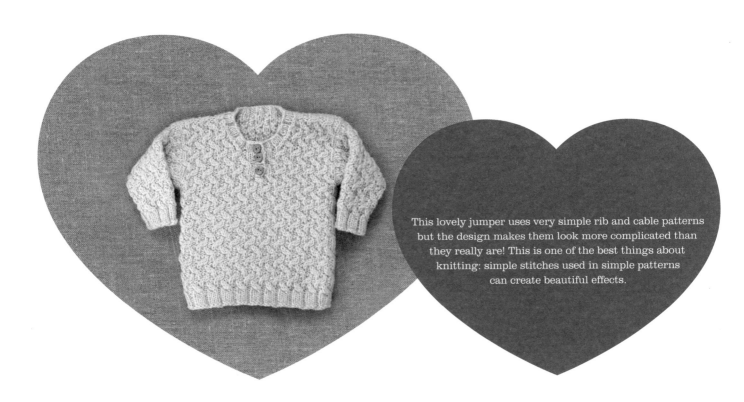

This lovely jumper uses very simple rib and cable patterns but the design makes them look more complicated than they really are! This is one of the best things about knitting: simple stitches used in simple patterns can create beautiful effects.

MATERIALS

2(3:3:4:4) 100g hanks of dk weight yarn.
(this amount is based on dk weight
yarn with 225m per 100g)
Pair of 3.75mm knitting needles.
Pair of 4mm knitting needles.
3(3:4:4:4) buttons.

TENSION

25 stitches and 30 rows to 10cm/4ins square
over cable pattern using 4mm needles.

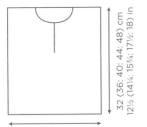

32 (36: 40: 44: 48) cm
12½ (14¼: 15¾: 17½: 18) in

26 (28.5: 31: 33.5: 36) cm
10¼: (11¼: 12¼: 13¼: 14¼) in

18 (22: 26: 30: 36) cm
7 (8¾: 10¼: 11¾: 14¼) in

14 (19: 21.5: 24: 24) cm
5½ (7½: 8½: 9½: 9½) in

MEASUREMENTS

to fit (suggested age)	0-1	1-2	3-4	5-6	7-8	yrs
actual chest measurement	**52**	**57**	**62**	**67**	**72**	**cm**
	20½	22½	24½	26¼	28¼	ins
length	**32**	**36**	**40**	**44**	**48**	**cm**
	12½	14¼	15¾	17½	18	ins
sleeve length	**18**	**22**	**26**	**30**	**36**	**cm**
	7	8¾	10¼	11¾	14¼	ins

back

With 3.75mm needles, cast on 55(60:65:70:75) stitches.
1st rib row (right side): k1, [k3, p2]to last 4 stitches, k4.
2nd rib row: p1, [p3, k2]to last 4 stitches, p4.
These 2 rows form the rib pattern.
Repeat the last 2 rows twice more.
Increase row (right side): k1, [k1, m1, k2, p2]to last 4 stitches, k1, m1, k3. 66(72:78:84:90) stitches
Next row: p1, [p4, k2]to last 5 stitches, p5.
Change to 4mm needles.
1st row (right side): k1, [C4F, p2]to last 5 stitches, C4F, k1.
2nd row: p1, [p4, k2]to last 5 stitches, p5.
3rd row: k2, [p2, k4]to last 4 stitches, p2, k2.
4th row: p2, [k2, p4]to last 4 stitches, k2, p2.
5th row: k2, [p2, C4B]to last 4 stitches, p2, k2.
6th row: as **4th row.**
7th row: k1, [k4, p2]to last 5 stitches, k5.
8th row: as **2nd row.**
These 8 rows form the cable pattern.
Repeat the last 8 rows until back measures approximately 32(36:40:44:48)cm/12½(14¼:15¾:17½:18)ins from cast on edge, ending with a **6th row.**

shape shoulders

Cast off 21(23:25:25:27) stitches at the beginning of the next 2 rows.
Leave centre 24(26:28:34:36) stitches on a holder.

front

Work as given for the back until front measures 12(12:14:14:14)cm/4¾(4¾:5½:5½:5½)ins less than the back (this will be approximately 20(24:26:30:34)cm/7¾(9½:10¼:11¾:13¼)ins from cast on edge), ending with a wrong side row.

shape left side

Next 2 rows: pattern 31(34:36:39:42) stitches, slip remaining 35(38:42:45:48) stitches onto a holder, turn and pattern to end. Continue without shaping in cable pattern until front measures 6cm/2¼ins less than the back, (this will be approximately 26(30:34:38:42)cm/10¼ (11¾:13¼):14¾:16½)ins from cast on edge), ending with a **right side row.**

shape left neck

Next row (wrong side): pattern 4(4:6:7:8) stitches, slip these stitches on a holder, pattern to end. 27(30:30:32:34) stitches
Neck decrease row (right side): pattern to last 3 stitches, k2tog, k1. 26(29:29:31:33) stitches
Decrease one stitch at neck edge on the next and every following alternate row until there are 21(23:25:25:27) stitches. Continue without shaping in cable pattern until front measures the same length as the back, ending with a wrong side row.
Cast off.

shape right side and neck

With right side facing, rejoin yarn to remaining 35(38:42:45:48) stitches, casting off centre 4(4:6:6:6) stitches, pattern to end. 31(34:36:39:42) stitches
Work as given for left side and neck, reversing shapings and working neck decreases as follows:
Neck decrease row (right side): k1, s1, k1, psso, pattern to end.

sleeves

With 3.75mm needles, cast on 30(40:45:50:50) stitches.
Starting with a **1st rib row** as given for the back, work as given for the back until sleeve measures 5cm/2¾ins from cast on edge, ending with a wrong side row. 36(48:54:60:60) stitches
Change to 4mm needles.
Starting with **1st row** of cable pattern as given for the back and keeping pattern correct, increase one stitch at each end on next and every following 4th row until there are 48(56:66:76:86) stitches. Continue without shaping in cable pattern until sleeve measures 18(22:26:30:36)cm/7(8¾:10¼:11¾:14¼)ins from cast on edge, ending with a wrong side row.
Cast off.

left side edging

With right side facing and 3.75mm needles, pick up and knit 10(10:15:15:15) stitches down left side edging.
1st row (wrong side): p1, [p3, k2]to last 4 stitches, p4.
2nd row: k1, [k3, p2] to last 4 stitches, k4.
3rd row: as **1st row.**
Cast off in pattern.

right side edging

With right side facing and 3.75mm needles, pick up and knit 10(10:15:15:15) stitches up right side edging.
1st row (wrong side): p1, [p3, k2]to last 4 stitches, p4.
Buttonhole row: k1, [k2tog, yon, k1, p2] to last 4 stitches, k2tog, yon, k2.
3rd row: as **1st row.**
Cast off in pattern.

neck edging

Join shoulder seams. With right side facing and 3.75mm needles, pick up and knit 3 stitches from right side edging, knit 4(4:6:7:8) from holder at right neck, pick up and knit 13(14:14:13:14) stitches up right front neck, work across the 24(26:28:34:36) stitches from holder at centre back as follows: p1(0:0:0:1), k1(0:0:0:1), k2[0:0:0:2]tog, k1(3:1:1:1), *p2, k1, k2tog, k1, repeat from * 3(3:4:5:5)times, p1(2:2:2:1), k0(3:1:1:0), then pick up and knit 13(14:14:13:14) stitches down left front neck, knit 4(4:6:7:8) from holder at left neck, pick up and knit 3 stitches from left side edging. 60(65:70:75:80) stitches
1st rib row: p4, [k2, p3]to last stitch, p1.
Buttonhole row (right side): k1, k2tog, yon, rib to end.
3rd rib row: as **1st rib row.**
Cast off in rib.

to make up

Sew on sleeves, placing centre of sleeves to shoulder seams. Join side and sleeve seams. Slip stitch edging ends into place with right edging over left edging. Position and sew buttons into place.

Bell Beck

Simple Garter Stitch Jumper

MATERIALS

2(2:3:3:4) 100g hanks of dk weight yarn.
(this amount is based on dk weight
yarn with 225m per 100g)
Pair of 4mm knitting needles.
2(2:4:4:4) buttons.

TENSION

22 stitches and 42 rows to 10cm/4ins square
over garter stitch using 4mm needles.

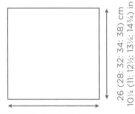

26 (28: 32: 34: 38) cm
10¼ (11: 12½: 13¼: 14¾) in

21.5 (26: 29: 32.5: 36) cm
8½ (10¼: 11½: 12¾: 14¼) in

15 (17: 20: 24: 28) cm
6 (6½: 7¾: 9½: 11) in

14.5 (16: 18: 20: 21.5) cm
5¾ (6¼: 7: 7¾: 8½) in

MEASUREMENTS

to fit (suggested age)	0-1	1-2	2-3	4-5	6-7	yrs
actual chest measurement	**43**	**52**	**58**	**65**	**72**	**cm**
	17	20½	22¾	25½	28¼	ins
length	**26**	**28**	**32**	**34**	**38**	**cm**
	10¼	11	12½	13¼	14¾	ins
sleeve length	**15**	**17**	**20**	**24**	**28**	**cm**
	6	6½	7¾	9½	11	ins

This little jumper is perfect for beginners or those knitting their first baby garment after a few years away from knitting.

Garter stitch is one of my favourite stitches, and one that is often overlooked for being 'too basic' when in fact it's the simplicity which makes it so beautiful, especially when knitted in a gorgeous yarn.

back

With 4mm needles, cast on 48(58:64:72:80) stitches.
Starting with a knit row, work in garter stitch until back measures 26(28:32:34:38)cm/10¼(11:12½:13¼:14¾)ins from cast on edge, ending with a wrong side row.
Knit 2 rows.
Cast off.

front

Work as given for the back until front measures 26(28:32:34:38)cm/ 10¼(11:12½:13¼:14¾)ins from cast on edge, ending with a wrong side row.
Buttonhole row (right side): [k4, k2tog, yon]1(1:2:2:2) time(s), knit to last 6(6:12:12:12) stitches, [yon, k2tog, k4]1(1:2:2:2) time(s).
Knit one row.
Cast off.

sleeves

With 4mm needles, cast on 32(36:40:44:48) stitches.
Starting with a knit row, work in garter stitch until sleeve measures 5cm/2ins from cast on edge, ending with a wrong side row.

Next row: k1, inc 1, knit to last 3 stitches, inc 1, k2.
34(38:42:46:50) stitches
This row sets the position of the increase stitches.
Knit 5 rows.
Increase one stitch at each end on next and every 6th row until there are 42(48:54:60:68) stitches.
Continue without shaping in garter stitch until sleeve measures 15(17:20:24:28)cm/6(6½:7¾:9½:11)ins from cast on edge, ending with a wrong side row.
Cast off.

to make up

Slip stitch the front buttonhole edging over the back at sleeve edge. Sew on sleeves, placing centre of sleeves to shoulder seams. Join side and sleeve seams. Position and sew buttons into place.

By Jane Ellison

Calton Gill Blanket
Striped Square Baby Blanket

One of the great things about this square blanket is that the squares are knitted individually so you can get a sense of satisfaction when you complete one. I like to stack the squares in piles, which look lovely and help you keep an eye on the progress you're making! Knitting the squares is a great way to relax because you can just do one or two rows in between other things or if you have a couple of minutes.

MATERIALS

Two 100g hanks in shade A.
One 100g hank each of shade B and shade C.
(this amount is based on yarn which has 225m per 100g. These make 30 squares in total, 15 squares with shade A & B and 15 squares with shades A & C.)
Pair of 4mm knitting needles.

TENSION

22 stitches and 42 rows to 10cm/4ins square over pattern using 4mm needles.

MEASUREMENTS

Each square is 17cm/6½ins x 17cm/6½ins.
The photographed blanket is made up of 5 x 6 squares, with the finished size of approximately 85cm/33½ins x 102cm/40¼ins

to make striped square

With 4mm needles and shade A, cast on 2 stitches.
Knit one row in shade A.
Starting with 1st row of striped pattern, work in striped pattern as follows:
Increase row: k1, inc 1, knit to end.
Keeping striped pattern correct, repeat the last row until there are 38 stitches.
Decrease row: knit to last 3 stitches, k2tog, k1.
Repeat last row until there are 2 stitches.
Knit one row.
Cast off.

striped pattern

Work 2 rows in shade B.
Work 2 rows in shade A.
These 4 rows form the striped pattern.

to make up

Work 15 squares in shades B and A.
Work another 15 squares in shades C and A, following the striped pattern but using shade C instead of shade B.
You can have fun and make up your blanket as you desire or to make the blanket as photographed alternate the squares making sure the diagonals of the stripes are at an angle to each other.

Lenny Jumper
Simple Garter Stitch Jumper

MATERIALS

3(3:4:4:5) 100g hanks of aran weight yarn.
(this amount is based on aran weight
yarn with 166m per 100g)
Pair of 5mm knitting needles.
One Button.

TENSION

17 stitches and 34 rows to 10cm/4ins square
over garter stitch using 5mm needles.

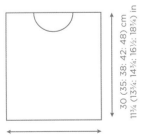

30 (35: 38: 42: 48) cm
11¾ (13¾: 14¾: 16½: 18¾) in

27 (29: 32.5: 35: 38.5) cm
10½ (11½: 12¾: 13¾: 15) in

18 (22: 26: 30: 36) cm
7 (8¾: 10¼: 11¾: 14¼) in

15 (17.5: 20: 22: 24.5) cm
6 (6¾: 7¾: 8¾: 9½) in

MEASUREMENTS

to fit (suggested age)	0-1	1-2	3-4	5-6	7-8	yrs
actual chest measurement	54	58	65	70	77	cm
	21¼	22¾	25½	27½	30¼	ins
length	30	35	38	42	48	cm
	11¾	13¾	14¾	16½	18¾	ins
sleeve length	18	22	26	30	36	cm
	7	8¾	10¼	11¾	14¼	ins

This lovely little jumper with a polo neck is perfect for beginners. It is in an aran weight yarn which means there are less stitches to cast on than there would be with a dk weight yarn.

It's great for keeping little ones warm when running about outside in autumnal weather. The garter stitch is calming too, so the perfect way for the knitter to sit and relax after long days trying to keep up with their little ones!

back

With 5mm needles, cast on 46(50:56:60:66) stitches.
Starting with a knit row, work in garter stitch until back measures 30(35:38:42:48)cm/11¾(13¾:14¾:16½:18¾)ins from cast on edge, ending with a wrong side row.

shape shoulders
Cast off 14(15:17:17:19) stitches at the beginning of the next 2 rows.
Leave centre 18(20:22:26:28) stitches on a holder.

front

Work as given for the back until front measures 24(29:32:36:42)cm/9½(11½:12½:14¼:16½)ins from cast on edge, ending with a wrong side row.

shape left neck
Next 2 rows: k18(19:21:21:23), slip remaining 28(31:35:39:43) stitches onto a holder, turn and knit to end.
Decrease row (right side): knit to last 4 stitches, k2tog, k2.
17(18:20:20:22) stitches
Knit one row.
Decrease one stitch at neck edge as set above on next and every following alternate row until there are 14(15:17:17:19) stitches.
Knit one row.
Continue without shaping in garter stitch until front measures 30(35:38:42:48)cm/11¾(13¾:14¾:16½:18¾)ins from cast on edge, ending with a wrong side row.
Cast off.

shape right neck
With right side facing, leave centre 10(12:14:18:20) stitches on a holder, rejoin yarn to remaining 18(19:21:21:23) stitches, knit to end.
Work to match left neck, working **Decrease row** as follows:
Decrease row (right side): k2, s1, k1, psso, knit to end.

sleeves

With 5mm needles, cast on 26(30:34:38:42) stitches.
Starting with a knit row, work in garter stitch until sleeve measures 4cm/1½in from cast on edge, ending with a wrong side row.
Next row: k1, inc 1, knit to last 3 stitches, inc 1, k2.
28(32:36:40:44) stitches
This row sets the position of the increase stitches.
Knit 3 rows.
Increase one stitch at each end on next and every 4th row until there are 40(44:48:54:58) stitches.
Continue without shaping in garter stitch until sleeve measures 18(22:26:30:36)cm/7(8¾:10¼:11¾:14¼)ins from cast on edge, ending with a wrong side row.
Cast off.

collar

Join right shoulder seam. With right side facing and 5mm needles, cast on 3 stitches, pick up and knit 12 stitches down left front neck, knit 10(12:14:18:20) stitches from holder at centre front, pick up and knit 12 stitches up right front neck, knit 18(20:22:26:28) stitches from holder at centre back, cast on 3 stitches.
58(62:66:74:78) stitches
Starting with a knit row, work in garter stitch until collar measures 2cm/¾ins, ending with a wrong side row.
Buttonhole row (right side): k1, k2tog, yon, knit to end.
Continue in garter stitch until collar measures 6cm/2¼ins, ending with a wrong side row.
Cast off.

to make up

Join left shoulder seam. Sew on sleeves, placing centre of sleeves to shoulder seams. Join side and sleeve seams. Slip stitch buttonhole side of collar on top of the other side of collar. Position and sew button into place.

Ghyllas Cardigan
Classic Garter Stitch Cardigan

MATERIALS

2(2:3:3:4) 100g hanks of dk weight yarn.
(this amount is based on dk weight
yarn with 225m per 100g)
Pair of 3.75mm knitting needles.
Pair of 4mm knitting needles.
5(5:6:7:7) buttons.

TENSION

22 stitches and 40 rows to 10cm/4ins square
over garter stitch using 4mm needles.

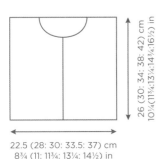

26 (30: 34: 38: 42) cm
10¼ (11¾: 13¼: 14¾: 16½) in

22.5 (28: 30: 33.5: 37) cm
8¾ (11: 11¾: 13¼: 14½) in

15 (17: 19: 20: 22) cm
6 (6½: 7½: 7¾: 8¾) in

15 (21: 25: 30: 36) cm
6 (8¼: 9¾: 11¾: 14¼) in

MEASUREMENTS

to fit (suggested age)	0-1	1-2	3-4	5-6	7-8	yrs
actual chest measurement	45	56	60	67	74	cm
	17¾	22	23½	26¼	29¼	ins
length	26	30	34	38	42	cm
	10¼	11¾	13¼	14¾	16½	ins
sleeve length	15	21	25	30	36	cm
	6	8¼	9¾	11¾	14¼	ins

By Jane Ellison

This classic cardigan is perfect for keeping your little one lovely and warm and comfortable and it's also perfect for you to knit. I hope you enjoy the soothing and relaxing rhythm of garter stitch as much as I do. I added rib at the edge of this cardigan because I love the combination of rib and garter stitch.

back

With 3.75mm needles, cast on 50(62:66:74:82) stitches.
1st row (right side): k2, [p2, k2]to end.
2nd row: p2, [k2, p2]to end.
These 2 rows form the rib.
Repeat the last 2 rows twice more, then work the **1st row** once more, ending with a **right side** row.
Change to 4mm needles.
Starting with a knit row, work in garter stitch until back measures 26(30:34:38:42)cm/10¼(11¾:13¼:14¾:16½)ins from cast on edge, ending with a wrong side row.

shape shoulders

Cast off 14(17:18:21:23) stitches at the beginning of the next 2 rows.
Leave centre 22(28:30:32:36) stitches on a holder.

left front

With 3.75mm needles, cast on 27(31:35:39:43) stitches.
1st row (right side): [k2, p2]to last 3 stitches, k3.
2nd row: p3, [k2, p2]to end.
These 2 rows form the rib.
Repeat the last 2 rows twice more, then work the **1st row** once more, ending with a **right side** row.
Change to 4mm needles.
Starting with a knit row, work in garter stitch until left front measures 20(24:28:32:36)cm/7¾(9½:11:12½:14¼)ins from cast on edge, ending with a **right side** row.

shape left neck

Next row (wrong side): k9(10:13:14:16), place these stitches on a holder, knit to end. 18(21:22:25:27) stitches
Decrease row (right side): knit to last 3 stitches, k2tog, k1.
17(20:21:24:26) stitches
Work one row.

Decrease one stitch at neck edge as set above on the next and every following alternate row until there are 14(17:18:21:23) stitches. Continue without shaping in garter stitch until left front measures 26(30:34:38:42)cm/10¼(11¾:13¼:14¾:16½)ins from cast on edge, ending with a wrong side row.
Cast off.

right front

With 3.75mm needles, cast on 27(31:35:39:43) stitches.
1st row (right side): k3, [p2, k2]to end.
2nd row: [p2, k2]to last 3 stitches, p3.
These 2 rows form the rib.
Repeat the last 2 rows twice more, then work the **1st row** once more, ending with a **right side** row.
Change to 4mm needles.
Starting with a knit row, work in garter stitch until right front measures 20(24:28:32:36)cm/7¾(9½:11:12½:14¼)ins from cast on edge, ending with a wrong side row.

shape right neck

Next row (right side): k9(10:13:14:16), place these stitches on a holder, knit to end. 18(21:22:25:27) stitches
Knit one row.
Decrease row (right side): k1, s1, k1, psso, knit to end.
17(20:21:24:26) stitches
Knit one row.
Decrease one stitch at neck edge as set above on the next and every following alternate row until there are 14(17:18:21:23) stitches. Continue without shaping in garter stitch until right front measures 26(30:34:38:42)cm/10¼(11¾:13¼:14¾:16½)ins from cast on edge, ending with a wrong side row.
Cast off.

sleeves

With 3.75mm needles, cast on 34(38:42:46:50) stitches.
Starting with a **1st row** as given for the back, work as given for the back until sleeve measures 5cm/2ins from cast on edge, ending with a wrong side row.
Change to 4mm needles.
Next row: k1, inc 1, knit to last 3 stitches, inc 1, k2. 36(40:44:48:52) stitches
This row sets the position of the increase stitches.
Knit 5 rows.
Increase one stitch at each end on next and every 6th row until there are 44(50:54:60:68) stitches.
Continue without shaping in garter stitch until sleeve measures 15(21:25:30:36)cm/6(8¼:9¾:11¾:14¼)ins from cast on edge, ending with a wrong side row.
Cast off.

buttonband left edging

Join shoulder seams. With right side facing and 3.75mm needles, pick up and knit 48(56:64:72:80) stitches down left front opening edge.
1st rib row (wrong side): p3, [k2, p2]to last stitch, p1.
2nd rib row: k3, [p2, k2]to last stitch, k1.
These 2 rows form the rib pattern.
Repeat the last 2 rows once more.
Then work the **1st rib row** once again.
Cast off in rib pattern.

buttonhole right edging

With right side facing and 3.75mm needles, pick up and knit 48(56:64:72:80) stitches up right front opening edge.
Starting with a **1st rib row** as given for **buttonband left edging**, work 2 rows in rib pattern.
Buttonhole row (wrong side): p3, k2(2:0:2:2), p2(2:0:2:2), k2(0:0:2:0), [p2tog, yon]1(0:0:1:0) time(s), *[k2, p2]twice, k2, p2tog, yon, repeat from * to last stitch, p1.
Work 2 rows in rib pattern.
Cast off in rib pattern.

neck edging

With right side facing and 3.75mm needles, pick up and knit 5 stitches from buttonhole right edging, knit 9(10:13:14:16) stitches from holder at right front, pick up and knit 15 stitches up right front neck, knit 22(28:30:32:36) stitches from holder at centre back, pick up and knit 15 stitches down left front neck, knit 9(10:13:14:16) stitches from holder at left front, pick up and knit 5 stitches from buttonband left edging. 80(88:96:100:108) stitches
Starting with a **1st rib row** as given for **buttonband left edging**, work 2 rows in rib pattern.
Buttonhole row (wrong side): rib to last 3 stitches, yon, p2tog, p1.
Work 2 rows in rib pattern.
Cast off in rib pattern.

to make up

Sew on sleeves, placing centre of sleeves to shoulder seams. Join side and sleeve seams. Position and sew buttons into place.

Strawberry Bank Cardigan
Delicate Ballet Crossover Cardigan

This lace cardigan is inspired by my niece who wanted a cardigan to wear for her ballet lessons.

In my patterns I always allow for knitters with different row tensions, however with this one some knitters might find the decrease rows just fit into the length because it's important to get the 30 rows. If you don't, do the fronts first and then work the back to match the length of the fronts.

On the neck edging, you pick up and then cast off, there isn't anything to do in-between those two instructions!

MATERIALS

1(2:2:2:3) 100g hanks of dk weight yarn.
(this amount is based on a dk weight
yarn with 225m per 100g)
One 3.75mm long circular needle.
Pair of 4mm knitting needles.

TENSION

22 stitches and 30 rows to 10cm/4ins square
over stocking stitch using 4mm needles.

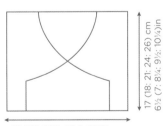

23 (26: 29.5: 32.5: 35.5) cm
9 (10¼: 11½: 12¾: 14) in

17 (18: 21: 24: 26) cm
6½ (7: 8¼: 9½: 10¼)in

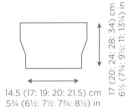

14.5 (17: 19: 20: 21.5) cm
5¾ (6½: 7½: 7¾: 8½) in

17 (20: 24: 28: 34) cm
6½ (7¾: 9½: 11: 13¼) in

MEASUREMENTS

to fit (suggested age)	0-1	1-2	3-4	5-6	7-8	yrs
actual chest measurement	**46**	**52**	**59**	**65**	**71**	**cm**
	18	20½	23¼	25½	27¾	ins
length	**17**	**18**	**21**	**24**	**26**	**cm**
	6½	7	8¼	9½	10¼	ins
sleeve length	**17**	**20**	**24**	**28**	**34**	**cm**
	6½	7¾	9½	11	13¼	ins

back

With 4mm needles, cast on 51(58:65:72:79) stitches.
Knit 2 rows.
1st row (right side): k2, [k2tog, yon, k1, yon, s1, k1, psso, k2]to end.
2nd row: purl to end.
3rd row: k1, [k2tog, yon, k3, yon, s1, k1, psso]to last stitch, k1.
4th row: purl to end.
These 4 rows form the lace pattern.
Repeat the last 4 rows 3(3:5:6:7) times more.
Starting with a knit row, work in stocking stitch until back measures 17(18:21:24:26)cm/6½(7:8¼:9½:10¼)ins from cast on edge, ending with a wrong side row.

shape shoulders

Cast off 14(16:18:19:21) stitches at the beginning of the next 2 rows.
Leave centre 23(26:29:34:37) stitches on a holder.

left front

With 4mm needles, cast on 37(44:51:58:65) stitches.
Knit 2 rows.
Starting with a **1st row** of lace pattern as given for the back, work in lace pattern until 16(16:24:28:32) rows of lace pattern have been worked.

shape left neck

Knit one row.
Next row (wrong side): p8(11:15:18:21), leave these 8(11:15:18:21) stitches on holder, purl to end. 29(33:36:40:44) stitches
Decrease row (right side): knit to last 3 stitches, k2tog, k1. 28(32:35:39:43) stitches
This row sets the position of the neck decreases.
Decrease one stitch at neck edge as set above on next and every following alternate row until there are 14(16:18:19:21) stitches. Continue without shaping in stocking stitch until left front measures 17(18:21:24:26)cm/6½(7:8¼:9½:10¼)ins from cast on edge ending with a wrong side row.
Cast off.

right front

Work as given for the left front until shape left neck.

shape right neck

Next row (right side): k8(11:15:18:21), leave theses 8(11:15:18:21) stitches on holder, knit to end. 29(33:36:40:44) stitches
Purl one row.

Decrease row (right side): k1, s1, k1, psso, knit to end. 28(32:35:39:43) stitches
This row sets the position of the neck decreases.
Decrease one stitch at neck edge as set above on next and every following alternate row until there are 14(16:18:19:21) stitches. Continue without shaping in stocking stitch until right front measures 17(18:21:24:26)cm/6½(7:8¼:9½:10¼)ins from cast on edge, ending with a wrong side row.
Cast off.

sleeves

With 4mm needles, cast on 32(38:42:44:48) stitches.
Starting with a knit row, work in stocking stitch until sleeve measures 3cm/1¼in from cast on edge, ending with a wrong side row.
Next row: k1, inc 1, knit to last 3 stitches, inc 1, k2. 34(40:44:46:50) stitches
This row sets the position of the increase stitches.
Work 5 rows in stocking stitch.
Increase one stitch at each end on next and every 6(6:6:4:4)th row until there are 42(48:54:60:68) stitches.
Continue without shaping in stocking stitch until sleeve measures 17(20:24:28:34)cm/6½(7¾:9½:11:13¼)ins from cast on edge, ending with a wrong side row.
Cast off.

edging and tie

Join shoulder seams. With right side facing and 3.75mm circular needle, cast on 48(48:52:52:56) stitches, knit 8(11:15:18:21) stitches from holder at right front edge, pick up and knit 27(29:31:35:39) stitches up right front edge, knit 23(26:29:34:37) stitches from holder at centre back, pick up and knit 27(29:31:35:39) stitches down left neck edging, knit 8(11:15:18:21) stitches from holder at left front edge, cast on 140(150:160:170:180) stitches. 281(304:333:362:393) stitches
Cast off.

to make up

Sew on sleeves, placing centre of sleeves to shoulder seams. Join side and sleeve seam. The longer left front tie can be thread through one of the lace holes on the inside of the right front and around the back to tie up with the shorter right front tie.

Strid Blanket
Simple Baby Blanket

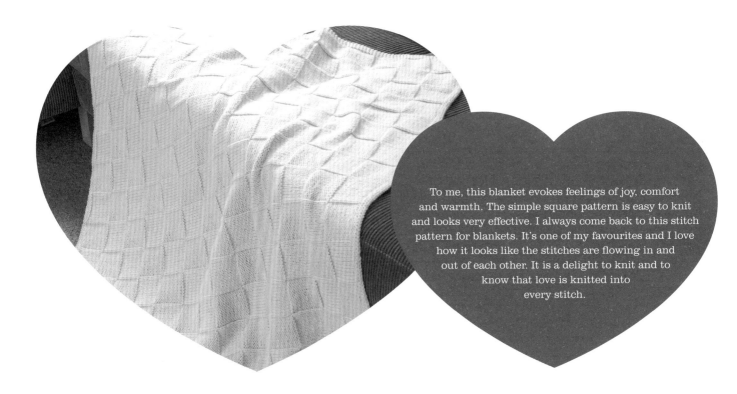

To me, this blanket evokes feelings of joy, comfort and warmth. The simple square pattern is easy to knit and looks very effective. I always come back to this stitch pattern for blankets. It's one of my favourites and I love how it looks like the stitches are flowing in and out of each other. It is a delight to knit and to know that love is knitted into every stitch.

MATERIALS

Six 100g hanks of aran weight yarn.
(this amount is based on aran weight yarn with 166m per 100g)
Pair of 5mm knitting needles.

TENSION

18 stitches and 24 rows to 10cm/4ins square over stocking stitch using 5mm needles.

MEASUREMENTS

104cm/40¾ins x approximately 100cm/39¼ins.

to make

With 5mm needles, cast on 188 stitches.
Knit 4 rows.
1st row (right side): k4, p12, [k12, p12]to last 4 stitches, k4.
2nd row: k16, [p12, k12]to last 4 stitches, k4.
Repeat the last 2 rows until 16 rows have been completed, ending with a wrong side row.
17th row (right side): as **2nd row**.
18th row: as **1st row**.
Repeat the last 2 rows until 16 rows have been completed, ending with a wrong side row.
These 32 rows form the pattern.

Repeat the last 32 rows until work measures approximately 96cm/37¾ins from cast on edge, ending with a **32nd row**.
Knit 4 rows.
Cast off.

to make up

Sew in ends neatly.

By Jane Ellison

Clapdale Hat

Cable Hat

I designed this hat based on my memories of a cable hat that my mother knitted for me when I was a baby. There are photos of me wearing it as a toddler and then photos of my younger sister wearing the same hat a few years later.

MATERIALS

One 100g hank of aran weight yarn.
(this amount is based on aran weight yarn with 166m per 100g)
Pair of 4mm knitting needles.
Pair of 4.5mm knitting needles.

TENSION

22 stitches and 38 rows to 10cm/4ins square over cable pattern using 4.5mm needles.

TO FIT (SUGGESTED)

Newborn, Baby, Child.

to make

With 4mm needles, cast on 72(82:92) stitches.
1st rib row (right side): p2, [k4, p2, k2, p2]to end.
2nd rib row: k2, [p2, k2, p4, k2]to end.
These 2 rows form the rib.
Repeat the last 2 rows twice more.
Change to 4.5mm needles.
Increase row (right side): p2, [k1, m1, k2, m1, k1, p2, k2, p2]to end. 86(98:110) stitches
Next row: k2, [p2, k2, p6, k2]to end.
1st row (right side): p2, [k2, C4F, p2, C2B, p2]to end.
2nd row (wrong side): k2, [p2, k2, p6, k2]to end.
3rd row: p2, [C4B, k2, p2, C2B, p2]to end.
4th row: as **2nd row**.
These 4 rows form the pattern.
Repeat the last 4 rows until hat measures 12(14:16)cm/4¾(5½:6¼)ins from cast on edge, ending with a wrong side row.
shape crown
1st decrease row: p2, [s1, k1, psso, CDF, p2, C2B, p2]to end. 65(74:83) stitches

Next row: k2, [p2, k2, p3, k2]to end.
2nd decrease row: p2tog, [k3, p2tog, C2B, p2tog]to end. 50(57:64) stitches
Next row: k1, [p2, k1, p3, k1]to end.
3rd decrease row: [k1, k2tog]twice, [k1, k2tog, k2, k2tog]to last 2 stitches, k2. 36(41:46) stitches
Purl one row.
4th decrease row: [k2tog]3 times, *k1, [k2tog]twice, repeat from * to end. 21(24:27) stitches
5th decrease row: [p2tog]to last stitch, p1(0:1). 11(12:14) stitches
6th decrease row: [k2tog]to last stitch, k1(0:0). 6(6:7) stitches
Break off yarn.
Thread through 6(6:7) stitches.
Pull securely and fasten off.

to make up

Sew side seam together.
Sew in ends neatly.
Make pom pom and secure to top of hat, if desired.

Cherry Tree Cardigan
Short Sleeved Garter Stitch Cardigan

MATERIALS

2(2:2:3:3) 100g hanks of dk weight yarn.
(this amount is based on a dk weight
yarn with 225m per 100g)
Pair of 4mm knitting needles.
One Button.

TENSION

22 stitches and 42 rows to 10cm/4ins square
over garter stitch using 4mm needles.

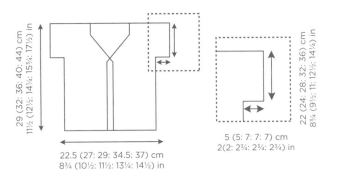

29 (32: 36: 40: 44) cm
11½ (12½: 14¼: 15¾: 17½) in

22.5 (27: 29: 34.5: 37) cm
8¾ (10½: 11½: 13¼: 14½) in

22 (24: 28: 32: 36) cm
8¾ (9½: 11: 12½: 14¼) in

5 (5: 7: 7: 7) cm
2(2: 2¾: 2¾: 2¾) in

MEASUREMENTS

to fit (suggested age)	0-1	1-2	3-4	5-6	7-8	yrs
actual chest measurement	45	54	58	69	74	cm
	17¾	21¼	22¾	27¼	29¼	ins
length	29	32	36	40	44	cm
	11½	12½	14¼	15¾	17½	ins
sleeve length	5	5	7	7	7	cm
	2	2	2¾	2¾	2¾	ins

This simple short sleeved cardigan is knitted by starting at the cast on edge of the fronts then up and over the shoulders and down the back - this beautifully limits the seams, with the only ones being the sleeve and side seams. To keep the garter stitch even when joining the fronts to the back, you knit one side and slip the other from the holders as the instructions. Also there are no pick up edges, so take extra care at the edges to keep them neat and join any new balls in at the side seams.

left front

With 4mm needles, cast on 29(33:37:42:45) stitches.
Starting with a knit row, work in garter stitch until left front measures 18(20:22:24:26)cm/7(7¾:8¾:9½:10¼)ins from cast on edge, ending with a wrong side row.

shape left sleeve

Cast on 12(12:16:16:16) stitches at the beginning of the next row, knit to end. 41(45:53:58:61) stitches
Knit one row.

shape left neck

Decrease row (right side): knit to last 4 stitches, k2tog, k2.
40(44:52:57:60) stitches
This row sets the position of the decrease stitch.
Knit one row.
Decrease one stitch at neck edge as set above on next and every following alternate row until there are 27(31:34:39:40) stitches.
Continue without shaping in garter stitch until sleeve measures 11(12:14:16:18)cm/4¼(4¾:5½:6¼:7)ins from start of sleeve shaping, ending with a wrong side row.
Leave all the stitches on a holder.

right front

With 4mm needles, cast on 29(33:37:42:45) stitches.
Work as given for the left front until right front measures 16(18:20:22:24)cm/6¼(7:7¾:8¾:9½)ins from cast on edge, ending with wrong side row.
Buttonhole row (right side): k2, s1, k1, psso, yon, knit to end.
Continue in garter stitch until right front measures 18(20:22:24:26)cm/ 7(7¾:8¾:9½:10¼)ins from cast on edge, ending with a **right side** row.

shape right sleeve

Cast on 12(12:16:16:16) stitches at the beginning of the next row, knit to end. 41(45:53:58:61) stitches

shape right neck

Decrease row (right side): k2, s1, k1, psso, knit to end.
40(44:52:57:60) stitches
This row sets the position of the decrease stitch.
Knit one row.
Decrease one stitch at neck edge as set above on next and every following alternate row until there are 27(31:34:39:40) stitches.
Continue without shaping in garter stitch until sleeve measures 11(12:14:16:18)cm/4¼(4¾:5½:6¼:7)ins from start of sleeve shaping, ending with a wrong side row.
Leave all the stitches on a holder.

back

With right sides facing and 4mm needles, knit across 27(31:34:39:40) stitches from left front holder, cast on 20(22:28:30:34) stitches and break yarn, slip 27(31:34:39:40) stitches from right front holder onto needle.
74(84:96:108:114) stitches.
Rejoin yarn and continue in garter stitch until sleeves measure 22(24:28:32:36)cm/8¾(9½:11:12½:14¼)ins from start of sleeve shaping on the fronts, ending with a wrong side row.

shape back sleeves

Cast off 12(12:16:16:16) stitches at the beginning of next two rows.
50(60:64:76:82) stitches.
Continue without shaping in garter stitch until back measures 18(20:22:24:26)cm/7(7¾:8¾:9½:10¼)ins from shape back sleeves, ending with a wrong side row.
Cast off.

to make up

Join side and sleeve seams.
Position and sew button into place.

Hazle Hooded Jacket
Simple Garter Stitch Jacket

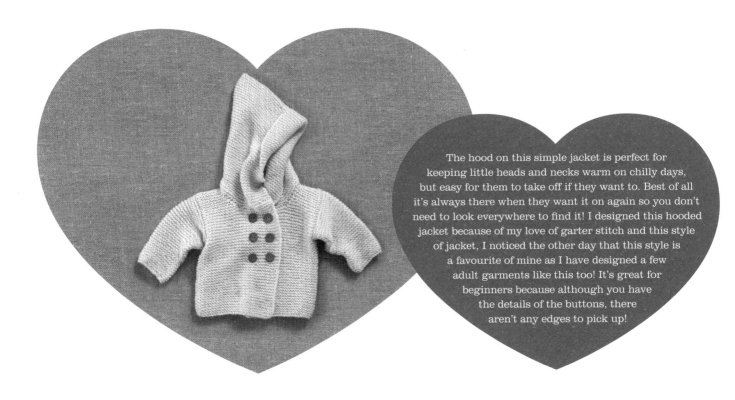

The hood on this simple jacket is perfect for keeping little heads and necks warm on chilly days, but easy for them to take off if they want to. Best of all it's always there when they want it on again so you don't need to look everywhere to find it! I designed this hooded jacket because of my love of garter stitch and this style of jacket, I noticed the other day that this style is a favourite of mine as I have designed a few adult garments like this too! It's great for beginners because although you have the details of the buttons, there aren't any edges to pick up!

MATERIALS

2(3:3:4:4) 100g hanks of dk weight yarn.
(this amount is based on dk weight
yarn with 225m per 100g)
Pair of 4mm knitting needles.
6 buttons.

TENSION

22 stitches and 40 rows to 10cm/4ins square
over garter stitch using 4mm needles.

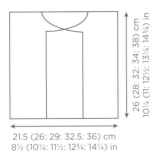

26 (28: 32: 34: 38) cm
10¼ (11: 12½: 13¼: 14¾) in

21.5 (26: 29: 32.5: 36) cm
8½ (10¼: 11½: 12¾: 14¼) in

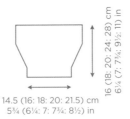

14.5 (16: 18: 20: 21.5) cm
5¾ (6¼: 7: 7¾: 8½) in

16 (18: 20: 24: 28) cm
6¼ (7: 7¾: 9½: 11) in

MEASUREMENTS

to fit (suggested age)	0-½	½-1	1-2	3-4	5-6	yrs
actual chest measurement	**43**	**52**	**58**	**65**	**72**	**cm**
	17	20½	22¾	25½	28¼	ins
length	**26**	**28**	**32**	**34**	**38**	**cm**
	10¼	11	12½	13¼	14¾	ins
sleeve length	**16**	**18**	**20**	**24**	**28**	**cm**
	6¼	7	7¾	9½	11	ins

back

With 4mm needles, cast on 48(58:64:72:80) stitches.
Starting with a knit row, work in garter stitch until back measures 26(28:32:34:38)cm/10¼(11:12½:13¼:14¾)ins from cast on edge, ending with a wrong side row.

shape shoulders

Cast off 13(16:18:20:22) stitches at the beginning of the next 2 rows.
Leave centre 22(26:28:32:36) stitches on a holder.

left front

With 4mm needles, cast on 32(39:42:48:54) stitches.
Starting with a knit row, work in garter stitch until left front measures 20(22:26:28:32)cm/7¾(8¾:10¼:11:12½)ins from cast on edge, ending with a **right side** row.

shape neck

Next row (wrong side): k16(20:21:25:29), slip these stitches on a holder, knit to end. 16(19:21:23:25) stitches
Decrease row (right side): knit to last 3 stitches, k2tog, k1.
15(18:20:22:24) stitches
Knit one row.
Decrease one stitch at neck edge as set above on next and following alternate row. 13(16:18:20:22) stitches
Continue without shaping in garter stitch until left front measures 26(28:32:34:38)cm/10¼(11:12½:13¼:14¾)ins from cast on edge, ending with a wrong side row.
Cast off.

right front

With 4mm needles, cast on 32(39:42:48:54) stitches.
Starting with a knit row, work in garter stitch until right front measures 10(12:16:18:22)cm/4(4¾:6¼:7:8¾)ins from cast on edge, ending with a wrong side row.
Buttonhole row: k3(3:3:4:5), k2tog, yon, k6(10:11:13:15), yon, k2tog, knit to end.
Continue in garter stitch until right front measures 14(16:20:22:26)cm/5½(6¼:7¾:8¾:10¼)ins from cast on edge, ending with a wrong side row.
Work **Buttonhole row** again.
Continue in garter stitch until right front measures 18(20:24:26:30)cm/7(7¾:9½:10¼:11¾)ins from cast on edge, ending with a wrong side row.
Work **Buttonhole row** again.
Continue in garter stitch until right front measures 20(22:26:28:32)cm/7¾(8¾:10¼:11:12½)ins from cast on edge, ending with a wrong side row.

shape neck

Next row (right side): k16(20:21:25:29), slip these stitches on a holder, knit to end. 16(19:21:23:25) stitches
Knit one row.
Decrease row (right side): k1, s1, k1, psso, knit to end.
15(18:20:22:24) stitches
Knit one row.
Decrease one stitch at neck edge as set above on next and following alternate row until there are 13(16:18:20:22) stitches.
Continue without shaping in garter stitch until right front measures 26(28:32:34:38)cm/10¼(11:12½:13¼:14¾)ins from cast on edge, ending with a wrong side row.
Cast off.

sleeves

With 4mm needles, cast on 32(36:40:44:48) stitches.
Starting with a knit row, work in garter stitch until sleeve measures 5cm/2ins from cast on edge, ending with a wrong side row.
Next row: k1, inc 1, knit to last 3 stitches, inc 1, k2.
34(38:42:46:50) stitches
This row sets the position of the increase stitches.
Knit 5 rows.
Increase one stitch at each end on next and every 6th row until there are 42(48:54:60:68) stitches.
Continue without shaping in garter stitch until sleeve measures 16(18:20:24:28)cm/6¼(7:7¾:9½:11)ins from cast on edge, ending with a wrong side row.
Cast off.

hood

Join shoulder seams. With right side facing and 4mm needles, slip 16(20:21:25:29) stitches from holder at right front onto needle, pick up and knit 18 stitches up right front neck, knit 22(26:28:32:36) stitches from holder at centre back, pick up and knit 18 stitches down left front neck, knit 16(20:21:25:29) stitches from holder at left front. 90(102:106:118:130) stitches
Starting with a knit row, work in garter stitch until hood measures 22(24:26:26:28)cm/8¾(9½:10¼:10¼:11)ins, ending with a wrong side row.
Cast off.

to make up

Fold hood in half and join cast off edge of hood. Sew on sleeves, placing centre of sleeves to shoulder seams. Join side and sleeve seams. Position and sew buttons into place.

Raydale Jumper
Boat Neck Simple Colourwork Jumper

MATERIALS

2(2:2:3:3) 100g hanks of aran weight
yarn in shade A and shade B.
(this amount is based on aran weight
yarn with 166m per 100g)
Pair of 5mm knitting needles.
4 buttons.

TENSION

20 stitches and 36 rows to 10cm/4ins square
over pattern using 5mm needles.

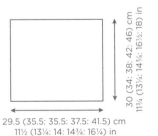

30 (34: 38: 42: 46) cm
11¾ (13¼: 13¾: 14¾: 18) in

29.5 (35.5: 35.5: 37.5: 41.5) cm
11½ (13¼: 14: 14¾: 16¼) in

18 (22: 26: 32: 38) cm
7 (8¾: 10¼: 12½: 14¾) in

21.5 (25.5: 27.5: 31.5: 35.5) cm
8½: 10: 10¾: 12¼: 14) in

MEASUREMENTS

to fit (suggested age)	1-2	3-4	5-6	7-8	9-10	yrs
actual chest measurement	**59**	**67**	**71**	**75**	**83**	**cm**
	23¼	26½	27¾	29½	32½	ins
length	**30**	**34**	**38**	**42**	**46**	**cm**
	11¾	13¼	14¾	16½	18	ins
sleeve length	**18**	**22**	**26**	**32**	**38**	**cm**
	7	8¾	10¼	12½	14¾	ins

54

I love hearing about individual knitting stories: how people started knitting, what their grandmothers, mothers, aunts used to knit and I hear tales of grandfathers, fathers and uncles knitting too. This jumper is inspired by fisherman jumpers, not perhaps the traditional Guernseys, but ones in my own family history where my relatives wore similar jumpers while living by the seaside and fishing for leisure.

To create a smooth stitch, I recommend that you s1 purlwise in this pattern.

back

With 5mm needles, cast on 59(67:71:75:83) stitches.
1st row (right side): with shade A, p1, [k1, p1]to end.
2nd row: with shade A, p1, k1, [p3, k1]to last stitch, p1.
3rd row: with shade B, p1, k1, p1, [ybk, s1, yfwd, p1, k1, p1]to end.
4th row: with shade B, p1, k1, p1, [s1, p1, k1, p1]to end.
These 4 rows form the pattern.
Repeat the last 4 rows until back measures approximately 29(33:37:41:45)cm/11½(13:14½:16¼:17¾)ins from cast on edge, ending with a **4th row**.
With shade A only, work 4 rows in pattern.
Cast off.

front

Work as given for the back until front measures approximately 29(33:37:41:45)cm/11½(13:14½:16¼:17¾)ins from cast on edge, ending with a **4th row**.
With shade A only, work 2 rows in pattern.
Buttonhole row: p1, k1, p1, [ybk, s1, k2tog, yon, p1, ybk, s1, yfwd, p1, k1, p1]2(2:2:3:3)times, pattern to last 16(16:16:24:24) stitches, [ybk, s1, yfwd, p1, yon, k2tog, s1, yfwd, p1, k1, p1]to end.
Work one row.
Cast off.

sleeves

With 5mm needles, cast on 43(51:55:63:71) stitches.
Work as given for the back until sleeve measures 18(22:26:32:38)cm/7(8¾:10¼:12½:14¾)ins from cast on edge, ending with a wrong side row.
Cast off.

to make up

Slip stitch the front buttonhole edgings over the back at sleeve edges. Sew on sleeves, placing centre of sleeves to shoulder seams. Join side and sleeve seams. Position and sew buttons into place.

Crag Jumper
Simple Cable Jumper

MATERIALS

3(4:4:5:5) 100g hanks of aran weight yarn.
(this amount is based on aran weight
yarn with 166m per 100g)
Pair of 4.5mm knitting needles.
Pair of 5mm knitting needles.
3 buttons.

TENSION

28 stitches and 26 rows to 10cm/4ins square over
middle cable pattern using 5mm needles.

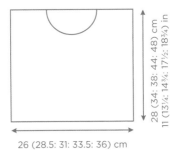

26 (28.5: 31: 33.5: 36) cm
10¼ (11¼: 12¼: 13¼: 14¼) in

28 (34: 38: 44: 48) cm
11 (13¼: 14¾: 17½: 18¾) in

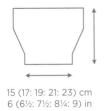

15 (17: 19: 21: 23) cm
6 (6½: 7½: 8¼: 9) in

18 (20: 24: 28: 36) cm
7 (7¾: 9½: 11: 14¼) in

MEASUREMENTS

to fit (suggested age)	0-1	1-2	3-4	5-6	7-8	yrs
actual chest measurement	52	57	62	67	72	cm
	20½	22½	24½	26¼	28¼	ins
length	28	34	38	44	48	cm
	11	13¼	14¾	17½	18¾	ins
sleeve length	18	20	24	28	36	cm
	7	7¾	9½	11	14¼	ins

By Jane Ellison

A simple cable looks so effective while at the same time being so exciting! In this design, I used two of my favourite cable patterns, one I call the honeycomb (I'm not sure if this is exactly the same as the 'official' one but it makes me think of bees and honey every time I see it) and the cable plait. This evokes feelings of childhood and plaiting my sister's hair (as well as cutting it but perhaps we shouldn't mention that here!).

back

With 4.5mm needles, cast on 64(72:76:84:88) stitches.

1st rib row (right side): [k2, p2]twice, k4, p2, k2, p3, [k2, p2]6(8:9:11:12) times, k2, p3, k2, p2, k4, [p2, k2]twice.

2nd rib row: [p2, k2]twice, p4, k2, p2, k3, p2, [k2, p2]6(8:9:11:12) times, k3, p2, k2, p4, [k2, p2]twice.

3rd rib row: k2, p2, C2B, p2, k4, p2, C2F, p3, [k2, p2]6(8:9:11:12) times, k2, p3, C2B, p2, k4, p2, C2F, p2, k2.

Repeat the last 2 rows once more.

Then work **2nd rib row** again.

Increase row (right side): k2, p2, C2B, p2, k1, m1, k2, m1, k1, p2, C2F, p3, m0(0:0:0:1), k2, m0(0:1:0:1), [p2, k2]0(1:0:0:0) time(s), [p2, k1, m1, k1]6(6:9:10:12) times, [p2, k2]0(1:0:1:0) time(s), p3, C2B, p2, k1, m1, k2, m1, k1, p2, C2F, p2, k2. 74(82:90:98:106) stitches

Next row (wrong side): [p2, k2]twice, p6, k2, p2, k3, p32(40:48:56:64), k3, p2, k2, p6, [k2, p2]twice.

Change to 5mm needles.

1st row (right side): p4, C2B, p2, k2, C4F, p2, C2F, p3, [C4B, C4F]4(5:6:7:8) times, p3, C2B, p2, k2, C4F, p2, C2F, p4.

2nd and every alternate row: k4, p2, k2, p6, k2, p2, k3, p32(40:48:56:64), k3, p2, k2, p6, k2, p2, k4.

3rd row: p4, C2B, p2, C4B, k2, p2, C2F, p3, k32(40:48:56:64), p3, C2B, p2, C4B, k2, p2, C2F, p4.

5th row: p4, C2B, p2, k2, C4F, p2, C2F, p3, [C4F, C4B]4(5:6:7:8) times, p3, C2B, p2, k2, C4F, p2, C2F, p4.

7th row: as **3rd row**.

These 8 rows form the pattern.

Repeat the last 8 rows until back measures 28(34:38:44:48)cm/11(13¼:14¾:17½:18¾)ins from cast on edge, ending with a wrong side row.

shape shoulders

Cast off 21(23:25:27:29) stitches at the beginning of the next row.

Leave remaining 53(59:65:71:77) stitches on a holder.

front

Work as given for the back until front measures approximately 22(28:32:38:42)cm/8¾(11:12½:14¾:16½)ins from cast on edge, ending with a wrong side row.

shape left neck

Next row (right side): pattern 25(27:29:32:33) stitches, turn and slip remaining 49(55:61:66:73) stitches onto a holder.

Work one row.

Decrease row: pattern to last 3 stitches, work2tog, work 1 stitch. 24(26:28:31:32) stitches

Work one row.

Decrease one stitch as set above at neck edge on the next and every following alternate row until there are 21(23:25:27:29) stitches.

Continue without shaping in pattern until front measures 28(34:38:44:48)cm/11(13¼:14¾:17½:18¾)ins from cast on edge, ending with a wrong side row.

buttonhole band

1st row (right side): p4, [k2, p2]to last 1(3:1:3:1) stitch(es), k0(3:0:3:0), p1(0:1:0:1).

2nd row (wrong side): p0(3:0:3:0), k3(2:3:2:3), [p2, k2]0(0:1:0:1) time, p2, k2tog, yon, p2, k2, p2, k2tog, yon, p2, [k2, p2]0(0:0:1:1) time, k4.

Work **1st row** once more.

Cast off.

shape right neck

With right side facing, leave centre 24(28:32:34:40) stitches on a holder, pattern to end.

Work as given for left neck, reversing shapings and working neck decrease as follows:

Decrease row (right side): work 1, s1, work 1, psso, work to end.

By Jane Ellison

sleeves

With 4.5mm needles, cast on 34(38:42:46:50) stitches.

1st rib row: k2, [p2, k2]to end.

2nd rib row: p2, [k2, p2]to end.

These 2 rows form the pattern.

Repeat the last 2 rows once more.

Increase row (right side): [k2, p2]1(2:2:3:3) time(s), [k1, m1, k1, p2]6 times, k2, [p2, k2]1(1:2:2:3) time(s). 40(44:48:52:56) stitches

Next row (wrong side): p2, k2, p0(2:0:2:0), p32(32:40:40:48), p0(2:0:2:), p2, k2.

Change to 5mm needles.

1st row (right side): p4(6:4:6:4), [C4B, C4F]4(4:5:5:6) times, p4(6:4:6:4).

2nd and every alternate row: k4(6:4:6:4), p32(32:40:40:48), k4(6:4:6:4).

3rd row: p4(6:4:6:4), k32(32:40:40:48), p4(6:4:6:4).

5th row: p4(6:4:6:4), [C4F, C4B]4(4:5:5:6) times, p4(6:4:6:4).

7th row: as **3rd row**.

These 8 rows form the pattern.

Keeping pattern correct and taking increase stitches into reverse stocking stitch, increase one stitch at each end on next and every following 4th row until there are 56(60:64:68:72) stitches.

Continue without shaping in pattern until sleeve measures 18(20:24:28:36)cm/7(7¾:9½:11:14¼)ins from cast on edge, ending with a wrong side row.

Cast off.

neck edging

Join right shoulder seam. With right side facing and 4.5mm needles, starting at buttonhole band edging pick up and knit 13 stitches down left front neck, work across the 24(28:32:34:40) stitches from holder at centre front follows: [k1, k2tog, p2] to last 4(3:2:4:0) stitches, k0(1:2:0:0), [k2tog]2(1:0:2:0) time(s), to make 18(22:26:26:30) stitches, pick up and knit 10 stitches up right front neck, work across 53(59:65:71:77) stitches as follows: k0(2:0:2:2) p0(2:0:2:2) [k1, k2tog, p2]6(6:8:8:10) times, k2(0:0:2:2), [k2tog]0(2:2:0:0) times, p0(0:0:2:0), k0(0:0:2:0), p2tog, p1, [k2, p2] to last 2 stitches, k2, to make 46(50:54:62:66) stitches. 87(95:103:111:119) stitches

1st rib row: p2, [k2, p2]to last 5 stitches, k2, p3.

Buttonhole row (right side): k1, k2tog, yon, rib to end.

Work **1st rib row** again.

Cast off in rib pattern.

to make up

Slip stitch buttonhole edging over back edging at shoulder. Sew on sleeves, placing centre of sleeves to shoulder seams. Join side and sleeve seams. Position and sew buttons into place.

Brockabank Jumper

Cable and Rib Jumper

I love this cable plait and try to use it wherever I can. This rib is another good one because I like to have a row off wherever possible – a row in the pattern where you can relax. In this rib, you have a knit row where you can relax, and in the cable you have the wrong side row where you don't cable so you can relax here too. I think knitting should be relaxing so this combination works perfectly!

MATERIALS

3(3:4:4:5) 100g hanks of aran weight yarn.
(this amount is based on aran weight
yarn with 166m per 100g)
Pair of 4.5mm knitting needles.
Pair of 5mm knitting needles.
3(3:3:4:4) buttons.

TENSION

19 stitches and 28 rows to 10cm/4ins square
over rib pattern using 5mm needles.
24 stitches and 32 rows to 10cm/4ins square over
cable pattern when stretched using 5mm needles.

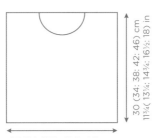

30 (34: 38: 42: 46) cm
11¾(13¼: 14¾: 16½: 18) in

31 (34: 37.5: 40.5: 44)cm
12¼: 13¼: 14¾: 16: 17½) in

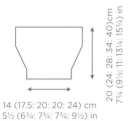

20 (24: 28: 34: 40)cm
7¾ (9½: 11: 13¼: 15¾) in

14 (17.5: 20: 20: 24) cm
5½ (6¾: 7¾: 7¾: 9½) in

MEASUREMENTS

to fit (suggested age)	1-2	3-4	5-6	7-8	9-10	yrs
actual chest measurement	**62**	**68**	**75**	**81**	**88**	cm
	24½	26¾	29½	31¾	34½	ins
length	**30**	**34**	**38**	**42**	**46**	cm
	11¾	13¼	14¾	16½	18	ins
sleeve length	**20**	**24**	**28**	**34**	**40**	cm
	7¾	9½	11	13¼	15¾	ins

By Jane Ellison

back

With 5mm needles, cast on 56(62:68:74:80) stitches.
Knit 2 rows.
1st rib row (right side): knit to end.
2nd rib row: k2, [p4, k2]to end.
These 2 rows form the rib pattern.
Repeat the last 2 rows until back measures 20(22:24:26:28)cm/
7¾(8¾:9½:10¼:11)ins from cast on edge, ending with a wrong
side row.
Increase row (right side): k2, [k1, m1, k2, m1, k3]to end.
74(82:90:98:106) stitches
Next row: k2, [p6, k2]to end.
1st row (right side): [k4, C4F]to last 2 stitches, k2.
2nd and every alternate row: k2, [p6, k2]to end.
3rd row: k2, [C4B, k4]to end.
These 4 rows form the cable pattern.
Repeat the last 4 rows until back measures 30(34:38:42:46)cm/
11¾(13¼:14¾:16½:18)ins from cast on edge, ending with a wrong
side row.

shape shoulders

Cast off 25(27:29:31:34) stitches at the beginning of the next row.
Leave 49(55:61:67:72) stitches on a holder.

front

Work as given for the back until front measures 24(28:32:36:40)cm/
9½(11:12½:14¼:15¾)ins from cast on edge, ending with wrong
side row.

shape left neck

Next 2 rows: pattern 28(30:32:34:37) stitches, turn and leave
remaining 46(52:58:64:69) stitches on a holder, pattern to end.
28(30:32:34:37) stitches
Neck decrease row (right side): pattern to last 3 stitches,
k2tog, k1. 27(29:31:33:36) stitches
Work one row.
Decrease one stitch at neck edge as set above on the
next and every following alternate row until there are
25(27:29:31:34) stitches.
Continue without shaping in cable pattern until front measures
29(33:37:41:45)cm/11½(13:14½:16¼:17¾)ins from cast on edge,
ending with a wrong side row.
Decrease row (right side): [k4, k2tog, k2]to last stitch, k1.
Buttonhole row (wrong side): k6, yon, k2tog,
[k5, yon, k2tog]1(1:1:2:2) times, knit to end.
Cast off with a knit row.

shape right neck

With right side facing, leave centre 18(22:26:30:32) stitches on a
holder, rejoin yarn to remaining 28(30:32:34:37) stitches, pattern
to end.

Neck decrease row (right side): k1, s1, k1, psso, pattern to end.
27(29:31:33:36) stitches
Work one row.
Decrease one stitch at neck edge as set above on the
next and every following alternate row until there are
25(27:29:31:34) stitches.
Continue without shaping in cable pattern until front measures
29(33:37:41:45)cm/11½(13:14½:16¼:17¾)ins from cast on edge,
ending with a wrong side row.
Work 2 rows.
Cast off.

sleeves

With 5mm needles, cast on 26(32:38:38:44) stitches
Starting with a **1st rib row** as given for the back, work 4 rows
in rib pattern, ending with a wrong side row.
Increase row (right side): k2, [k1, m1, k2, m1, k3]to end.
34(42:50:50:58) stitches
Next row: k2, [p6, k2]to end.
Starting with a **1st row** of cable pattern as given for the back and
keeping pattern correct, increase one stitch at each end on next
and every following 4th row until there are 52(60:68:68:76) stitches.
Continue without shaping in cable pattern until sleeve measures
20(24:28:34:40)cm/7¾(9½:11:13¼:15¾)ins from cast on edge,
ending with a wrong side row.
Cast off.

neck edging

Join right shoulder seam. With right side facing and 4.5mm
needles, pick up and knit 15 stitches down left front neck, work
across the 18(22:26:30:32) stitches from holder at centre front as
follows: k0(0:4:2:1), k2(0:2:2:0)tog, [k6, k2tog]to last 0(6:4:2:7)
stitches, k0(6:4:2:7), to make 15(20:23:26:29) stitches, then
pick up and knit 13 stitches up right front neck, work across
the 49(55:61:67:72) stitches from holder at back as follows:
k3(1:1:5:2), k2(2:0:2:2)tog, [k6, k2tog]to last 4 stitches, k4, to make
43(48:53:59:63) stitches. 87(96:105:113:120) stitches
Knit one row.
Buttonhole row (right side): k1, yon, k2tog, knit to end.
Cast off on wrong side row.

to make up

Slip stitch buttonhole edging over back edging at shoulder. Sew
on sleeves, placing centre of sleeves to shoulder seams. Join side
and sleeve seams. Position and sew buttons into place.

Danny Brow Jumper
Striped Ridge Jumper

MATERIALS

1(1:2:2:2) 100g hank(s) each of dk weight
yarn in shade A, shade B and shade C.
(this amount is based on dk weight
yarn with 225m per 100g)
Pair of 3.75mm knitting needles.
Pair of 4mm knitting needles.

TENSION

20 stitches and 42 rows to 10cm/4ins square
over ridge pattern using 4mm needles.

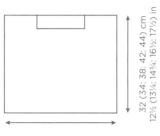

32 (34: 38: 42: 44) cm
12½ (13¼: 14¾: 16½: 17½) in

39 (41: 43: 45: 47) cm
15¼ (16¼: 17: 17¾: 18½) in

18 (22: 26: 30: 38) cm
7 (8¾: 10¼: 11¾: 14¾) in

16 (17: 18: 20: 22) cm
6¼ (6½: 7: 7¾: 8¾) in

MEASUREMENTS

to fit (suggested age)	1-2	3-4	5-6	7-8	9-10	yrs
actual chest measurement	78	82	86	90	94	cm
	30¾	32¼	33¾	35½	37	ins
length	32	34	38	42	44	cm
	12½	13¼	14¾	16½	17½	ins
sleeve length	18	22	26	30	38	cm
	7	8¾	10¼	11¾	14¾	ins

This simple striped jumper really puts the jump in jumper! The ridges seem to bounce up and down as the wearer jumps about in piles of autumn leaves. There are a few things to keep in mind when knitting this: when measuring the length, don't stretch it too much…but do bear in mind it will drop a little after washing. Also this garment is designed to be very oversized, however as with all hand knitted things, choose the right one for you.

striped pattern

Work 2 rows in shade A.
Work 4 rows in shade B.
Work 2 rows in shade A.
Work 4 rows in shade C.
These 12 rows form the striped pattern.

ridge pattern

1st row (right side): knit to end.
2nd row: purl to end.
3rd and 4th rows: knit to end.
5th row: purl to end.
6th row: knit to end.
These 6 rows form the ridge pattern.

back

With 4mm needles and shade A, cast on 78(82:86:90:94) stitches. Knit 2 rows.
Starting with the **1st row** of striped pattern and **1st row** of ridge pattern, work in striped pattern and ridge pattern until back measures 32(34:38:42:44)cm/12½(13¼:14¾:16½:17½)ins from cast on edge, ending with a wrong side row.

shape shoulders

Cast off 26(27:28:29:30) stitches at the beginning of the next 2 rows.
Leave remaining 26(28:30:32:34) stitches on a holder.

front

Work as given for the back until front measures 28(30:34:38:40)cm/11(11¾:13¼:14¾:15¾)ins from cast on edge, ending with a wrong side row.

shape left neck

Next 2 rows: pattern 26(27:28:29:30) stitches, slip remaining 52(55:58:61:64) stitches on a holder, turn and pattern to end.
Continue without shaping in striped pattern and ridge pattern until front measures 32(34:38:42:44)cm/12½(13¼:14¾:16½:17½)ins from cast on edge, ending with a wrong side row.
Cast off.

shape right neck

With right side facing, leave centre 26(28:30:32:34) stitches on a holder, rejoin yarn to remaining 26(27:28:29:30) stitches, pattern to end.
Work as given for left neck.

sleeves

With 4mm needles and shade A, cast on 32(34:36:40:44) stitches. Knit 2 rows.
Starting with the **1st row** of striped pattern and **1st row** of ridge pattern, work in striped pattern and ridge pattern until sleeve measures 3cm/1¼ins from cast on edge, ending with a wrong side row.
Keeping pattern correct, increase one stitch at each end on next and every following 6th row until there are 46(48:50:54:58) stitches.
Continue without shaping in pattern until sleeve measures 18(22:26:30:38)cm/7(8¾:10¼:11¾:14¾)ins from cast on edge, ending with a wrong side row.
Cast off.

neck edging

Join right shoulder seam. With right side facing, 3.75mm needles and yarn A, pick up and knit 12 stitches down left front neck, knit 26(28:30:32:34) stitches from holder at centre front, pick up and knit 12 stitches up right front neck, knit 26(28:30:32:34) stitches from holder at back. 76(80:84:88:92) stitches
Knit 2 rows.
Cast off on wrong side row.

to make up

Join left shoulder seam and neck edging. Sew on sleeves, placing centre of sleeves to shoulder seams. Join side and sleeve seams.

By Jane Ellison

Gamsber

Ribbed Raglan Jumper

MATERIALS

2(3:3:4) 100g hanks of dk weight yarn.
(this amount is based on dk weight
yarn with 225m per 100g)
Pair of 3.75mm knitting needles.
Pair of 4mm knitting needles.

TENSION

28 stitches and 34 rows to 10cm/4ins square
over rib pattern using 4mm needles.

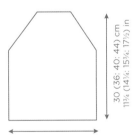

30 (36: 40: 44) cm
11¾ (14¼: 15¾: 17½) in

26.5 (29.5: 32.5: 35) cm
10½ (11½: 12¾: 13¾) in

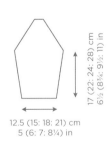

17 (22: 24: 28) cm
6½ (8¾: 9½: 11) in

12.5 (15: 18: 21) cm
5 (6: 7: 8¼) in

MEASUREMENTS

to fit (suggested age)	0-1	1-2	3-4	5-6	yrs
actual chest measurement	**53**	**59**	**65**	**70**	**cm**
	21	23¼	25½	27½	ins
length	**30**	**36**	**40**	**44**	**cm**
	11¾	14¼	15¾	17½	ins
sleeve length	**17**	**22**	**24**	**28**	**cm**
	6½	8¾	9½	11	ins

I love this rib pattern. It's so simple, yet it looks so effective. I've set the position of the decrease on the raglans one stitch in from the edge, and then on the wrong side these edge two stitches are purl to create a lovely smooth edge - which makes sewing up much easier. There is a tricky moment when picking up the stitches for the neck: I like it when the stitch pattern continues smoothly into the collar.

back and front alike

With 4mm needles, cast on 75(83:91:99) stitches.
1st rib row (right side): [k3, p1]to last 3 stitches, k3.
2nd rib row: p2, [k3, p1]to last stitch, p1.
These 2 rows form the rib pattern.
Repeat the last 2 rows until back measures 20(24:26:28)cm/ 7¾(9½:10¼:11)ins from cast on edge, ending with a wrong side row.

shape raglans

Cast off 4 stitches at the beginning of the next 2 rows. 67(75:83:91) stitches
Decrease row (right side): k1, s1, k1, psso, pattern to last 3 stitches, k2tog, k1. 65(73:81:89) stitches
Next row (wrong side): p2, pattern to last 2 stitches, p2.
These rows set the position of the raglan decrease stitches.
Decrease one stitch at each armhole edge as set above on next and every alternate row until there are 33(35:37:37) stitches.
Leave centre 33(35:37:37) stitches on a holder.

sleeves

With 4mm needles, cast on 35(43:51:59) stitches.
Starting with a **1st rib row** as given for the back, work as given for the back until sleeve measures 3cm/2¾ins from cast on edge, ending with a wrong side row.
Keeping pattern correct, increase one stitch at each end on next and every following 2nd(4th:4th:4th) row until there are 59(67:75:83) stitches.
Continue without shaping in rib pattern until sleeve measures 17(22:24:28)cm/6½(8¾:9½:11)ins from cast on edge, ending with a wrong side row.

shape raglans

Cast off 4 stitches at the beginning of the next 2 rows. 51(59:67:75) stitches
Decrease row (right side): k1, s1, k1, psso, pattern to last 3 stitches, k2tog, k1. 49(57:65:73) stitches
Next row (wrong side): p2, pattern to last 2 stitches, p2.
These rows set the position of the raglan decrease stitches.
Decrease one stitch at each edge as set above on next and every alternate row until there are 17(19:21:21) stitches.
Leave these 17(19:21:21) stitches on a holder.

collar

Join raglan seams leaving back left seam open. With right side facing and 3.75mm needles, work across 17(19:21:21) stitches from holder at left sleeve as follows: pattern to last 2(3:2:2) stitches, k2(3:2:2)togtbl, work across 33(35:37:37) stitches from centre front as follows: k0(2:0:0)togtbl, pattern to last 2(3:2:2) stitches, k2(3:2:2)tog, work across 17(19:21:21) stitches from holder at right sleeve as follows: k0(2:0:0)tog, pattern to last 2(3:2:2) stitches, k2(3:2:2)togtbl, work across 33(35:37:37) stitches from holder at centre back as follows: k0(2:0:0)togtbl, pattern to last 0(2:0:0) stitches, k0(2:0:0)tog. 97(99:113:113) stitches
Continue in pattern until collar measures 5cm/2ins, ending on a wrong side row.
Cast off in pattern.

to make up

Sew up back left raglan seam and collar. Join side and sleeve seams.

Hanlith Hat

Garter Stitch Hat

This hat is knitted in my favourite stitch and simply made into a hat. I designed this one for new knitters that wanted to progress on from knitted squares or scarves. This is ideal because it is still knitted straight up - until the last few rows and then you can practise decreasing. For more experienced knitters I feel it is the perfect weekend project. For everyone it is the perfect gift, a hand knitted accessory in a favourite shade of a gorgeous yarn to keep the recipient feeling warm and happy.

MATERIALS
One 100g hank of dk weight yarn.
(this amount is based on dk weight
yarn with 225m per 100g)
Pair of 4mm knitting needles.

TENSION
22 stitches and 44 rows to 10cm/4ins square
over garter stitch using 4mm needles.

TO FIT (SUGGESTED)
Newborn, Baby, Child.

to make

With 4mm needles, cast on 70(80:90) stitches.
Starting with a knit row, work in garter stitch until hat measures 12(15:18)cm/4¾(6:7)ins from cast on edge, ending with a wrong side row.

shape crown
1st decrease row: [k4, k2tog, k4]to end. 63(72:81) stitches
Next row: knit to end.
2nd decrease row: [k3, k2tog, k4]to end. 56(64:72) stitches
Next row: knit to end.
3rd decrease row: [k2, k2tog, k4]to end. 49(56:63) stitches
Next row: knit to end.
4th decrease row: [k1, k2tog, k4]to end. 42(48:54) stitches
Next row: knit to end.
5th decrease row: k6, [k2tog, k4]to end. 36(41:46) stitches
Next row: knit to end.
6th decrease row: k5, [k2tog, k3]to last stitch, k1.
30(34:38) stitches

Next row: knit to end.
7th decrease row: k4, [k2tog, k2]to last 2 stitches, k2.
24(27:30) stitches
Next row: knit to end.
8th decrease row: k3, [k2tog, k1]to end. 17(19:21) stitches
Next row: knit to end.
9th decrease row: [k2tog]to last stitch, k1. 9(10:11) stitches
Next row: knit to end.
10th decrease row: k1(0:1), [k2tog]to end. 5(5:6) stitches
Break off yarn.
Thread through 5(5:6) stitches.
Pull securely and fasten off.

to make up

Sew up side seam.
Sew in ends neatly.
Make pom pom and secure to top of hat, if desired.

By Jane Ellison

Hawking Pots Blanket
Circle Cable Baby Blanket

I designed all my blankets so that they don't have a 'wrong side'. This means that when you and/or your little one are wrapped up in them it doesn't matter which side is on show because both look good. This is one of the reasons why I love this cable pattern, it is the same on both sides!

MATERIALS

Five 100g hanks of aran weight yarn.
(this amount is based on aran weight yarn with 166m per 100g)
Pair of 5mm knitting needles.

TENSION

26 stitches and 24 rows to 10cm/4ins square over cable pattern using 5mm needles.

SIZE

54cm/21¼ins x approximately 102cm/40¼ins.

to make

With 5mm needles, cast on 142 stitches.
Knit four rows.
1st row (right side): k3, p2, k4, [p4, k4]to last 5 stitches, p2, k3.
2nd row (wrong side): k5, p4, [k4, p4]to last 5 stitches, k5.
3rd row: k3, [T4B, T4F]to last stitch, k3.
4th row: as **1st row**.
5th row: as **2nd row**.
6th row: as **1st row**.
7th row: k3, [T4F, T4B]to last 3 stitches, k3.
8th row: as **2nd row**.

These 8 rows form the cable pattern.
Repeat the last 8 rows until blanket measures 100cm/39¼ins from cast on edge, ending with a **8th row**.
Knit four rows.
Cast off.

Sepperdin Blanket
Chevron Stitch Baby Blanket

The chevron stitch pattern is one of my favourites because I love how this simple two row pattern, combined with a striped pattern, creates this amazing zig zag. It epitomises everything I love about knitting. Simple stitch, simple stripe, simply beautiful.

MATERIALS

Two 100g hanks each of aran weight yarn in shades A, B and C.
(this amount is based on aran weight yarn with 166m per 100g)
Pair of 5mm knitting needles.

striped pattern

1st row: with shade B, work one row.
2nd row: with shade C, work one row.
3rd row: with shade A, work one row.
These 3 rows form the striped pattern.

chevron pattern

1st row (right side): k1, [yon, k4, s1, k2tog, psso, k4, yon, k1]to end.
2nd row: knit to end.
These 2 rows form the chevron pattern.

TENSION

22 stitches and 22 rows to 10cm/4ins square over pattern using 5mm needles.

MEASUREMENTS

Approximately 50cm/19¾ins x approximately 121cm/47½ins.

to make

With 5mm needles and shade A, cast on 109 stitches.
Knit one row.
Starting with the **1st row** of striped pattern and **1st row** of chevron pattern, work in striped and chevron pattern until blanket measures approximately 120cm/47¼ins from cast on edge, ending with a **3rd row** of striped pattern and **1st row** of chevron pattern.
Continue in shade A only.
Knit one row.
Cast off.

Cringley Baby Sock

Ribbed Sock

MATERIALS

One 100g hank of dk weight yarn.
(this amount is based on dk weight
yarn with 225m per 100g)
Set of double pointed 3.25mm knitting needles.

TENSION

24 stitches and 32 rows to 10cm/4ins square
over stocking stitch using 3.25mm needles.

TO FIT (SUGGESTED)

1-2 year old (see my comments on how to
make this sock fit older children)

By Jane Ellison

I love this little sock. It's the perfect sock for your little ones to wear under wellies to keep their feet warm as they play in the snow or jump in puddles.

This is a magical sock and the cast on amount will fit children up to the age of 5 years old, the only bit to change to get the length correct for your child's foot is the bit in shape instep where it says ...'until foot measures 6cm/2¼ins (or your desired length)'. Here you knit until you reach the length of your child's foot from the ankle to about 2.5cm/1in from end of toes.

to make

With 3.25mm double pointed needles, cast on 36 stitches.
Distribute stitches evenly onto 3 needles as follows: 12 on first needle, 12 on second needle and 12 on third needle.
12-12-12 stitches
Work in rounds as follows:
Rib round: [k2, p2] to end.
This round forms the rib pattern.
Repeat the last round until sock measures 12cm/4¾ins from cast on edge.

shape heel

Pattern 7 stitches from first needle and slip last 9 stitches from third needle onto end of first needle.
These 16 stitches are for the heel. Leave the remaining 20 stitches on one needle for instep.
Working in rows and starting with a wrong side row, work as follows:
1st row (wrong side): p3, [k2, p2]to last stitch, p1.
2nd row (right side): k3, [p2, k2]to last stitch, k1.
Repeat the last 2 rows until 10 rows have been completed.
Work the **1st row** once more.

turn heel

Next row (right side): k10, s1, k1, psso, turn.
1st row (wrong side): s1, p4, p2tog, turn.
2nd row: s1, k4, s1, k1, psso, turn.
Repeat the last 2 rows 3 times more, then the **1st row** once more.
Next row: k3 (thus completing heel)
Using first needle, knit 3 stitches from heel, pick up and knit 11 stitches up one side of heel.

Using second needle p1, k2, [p2, k2]4 times, p1 across 20 instep stitches.
Using third needle pick up and knit 11 stitches down other side of heel and remaining 3 stitches of heel. 14-20-14 stitches

shape instep

Work in rounds as follows:
1st round: 1st needle - knit to last stitch, p1. **2nd needle** – p1, k2, [p2, k2]4 times, p1. **3rd needle** – p1, knit to end.
2nd round: 1st needle - knit to last 3 stitches, k2tog, p1.
2nd needle – p1, k2, [p2, k2]4 times, p1. **3rd needle** – p1, s1, k1, psso, knit to end.
Repeat the last 2 rounds until there are 40 stitches.
10-20-10 stitches
Repeat the **1st round** only until foot measures 6cm/2¼ins (or your desired length) from the start of instep shaping.

shape toe

Next round: 1st needle - knit to last 3 stitches, k2tog, k1.
2nd needle - k1, s1, k1, psso, knit to last 3 stitches, k2tog, k1.
3rd needle - k1, s1, k1, psso, knit to end.
Next round: knit.
Repeat the last 2 rounds until there are 20 stitches. 5-10-5 stitches
Knit 5 stitches from first needle onto end of third needle.
10-10 stitches
Graft stitches together.

to make up

Sew in ends neatly.

By Jane Ellison

Oxenber Tank Top
Cable V-neck Tank Top

MATERIALS

1(1:2:2:3) 100g hank(s) of dk weight yarn.
(this amount is based on dk weight
yarn with 225m per 100g)
Pair of 3.75mm knitting needles.
Pair of 4mm knitting needles.

TENSION

22 stitches and 32 rows to 10cm/4ins square over
rib pattern when stretched using 4mm needles.

24 (28: 34: 40: 46) cm
9½ (11: 13¼: 15¾: 8) in

21 (25: 29: 33: 37) cm
8¼ (9¾: 11½: 13: 14½) ins

MEASUREMENTS

to fit (suggested age)	0-1	1-2	3-4	5-6	7-8	yrs
actual chest measurement	42	50	58	66	74	cm
	16½	19¾	22½	26	29¼	ins
length	24	28	34	40	46	cm
	9½	11	13¼	15¾	18	ins

By Jane Ellison

I love playing about, designing with ribs and
cables. I also enjoy playing with decreases, making
sure the stitches follow the line of decreases smoothly.
I think I knitted this 'simple' little tank top about four or
five times to get the detail exactly right. I wanted the cables
to follow up and over and down the back so I had to make
sure the rib pattern was the correct repeat. This
pattern was definitely one that challenged my
designer's mind! I wanted it to be simple
and easy to knit so there aren't any
edges to pick up – remember this
when joining in new balls.

back

With 3.75mm needles, cast on 50(59:72:85:98) stitches.
1st rib row: p2(0:2:0:2), k3(5:3:5:3), p2, k0(0:2:3:4), p0(0:2:2:2),
k3(4:2:3:4), p1, k3(4:2:3:4), p0(0:2:2:2), k0(0:2:3:4), p2, [k3,
p2]4(5:6:7:8) times, k0(0:2:3:4), p0(0:2:2:2), k3(4:2:3:4), p1,
k3(4:2:3:4), p0(0:2:2:2), k0(0:2:3:4), p2, k3(5:3:5:3), p2(0:2:0:2).
2nd rib row: k2(0:2:0:2), p3(5:3:5:3), k2, p0(0:2:3:4), k0(0:2:2:2),
p3(4:2:3:4), k1, p3(4:2:3:4), k0(0:2:2:2), p0(0:2:3:4), k2, [p3,
k2]4(5:6:7:8) times, p0(0:2:3:4), k0(0:2:2:2), p3(4:2:3:4), k1,
p3(4:2:3:4), k0(0:2:2:2), p0(0:2:3:4), k2, p3(5:3:5:3), k2(0:2:0:2).
These 2 rows form the rib pattern.
Repeat the last 2 rows 1(1:2:3:4) times more.
Increase row (right side): p2(0:2:0:2), k3(5:3:5:3), p2, k1(1:1:2:3),
m1, k2(2:4:4:4), m0(1:1:1:1), k0(1:1:2:3), p1, k1(1:1:2:3), m1, k2(2:4:4:4),
m0(1:1:1:1), k0(1:1:2:3), [p2, k3]4(5:6:7:8) times, p2, k1(1:1:2:3), m1,
k2(2:4:4:4), m0(1:1:1:1), k0(1:1:2:3), p1, k1(1:1:2:3), m1, k2(2:4:4:4),
m0(1:1:1:1), k0(1:1:2:3), p2, k3(5:3:5:3), p2(0:2:0:2).
54(67:80:93:106) stitches
Change to 4mm needles.
Next row: k2(0:2:0:2), p3(5:3:5:3), k2, p4(6:8:10:12), k1, p4(6:8:10:12),
k2, [p3, k2]4(5:6:7:8) times, p(6:8:10:12), k1, p4(6:8:10:12), k2,
p3(5:3:5:3), k2(0:2:0:2).
1st row: p2(0:2:0:2), k3(5:3:5:3), p2, C4(6:8:10:12)B, p1,
C4(6:8:10:12)F, [p2, k3]4(5:6:7:8) times, p2, C4(6:8:10:12)B, p1,
C4(6:8:10:12)F, p2, k3(5:3:5:3), p2(0:2:0:2).
2nd and every alternate row: k2(0:2:0:2), p3(5:3:5:3), k2,
p4(6:8:10:12), k1, p4(6:8:10:12), k2, [p3, k2]4(5:6:7:8) times,
p4(6:8:10:12), k1, p4(6:8:10:12), k2, p3(5:3:5:3), k2(0:2:0:2).
3rd row: p2(0:2:0:2), k3(5:3:5:3), p2, k4(6:8:10:12), p1, k4(6:8:10:12),
[p2, k3]4(5:6:7:8) times, p2, k4(6:8:10:12), p1, k4(6:8:10:12), p2,
k3(5:3:5:3), p2(0:2:0:2).

These 4 rows form the pattern.
Repeat the last 4 rows until back measures 14(16:20:24:28)cm/
5½(6¼:7¾:9½:11)ins from cast on edge, ending with a wrong
side row.
shape armholes
Cast off 3 stitches at the beginning of the next 2 rows.
48(61:74:87:100) stitches
Decrease one stitch at armhole edge on next and every following
4th row until there are 42(55:68:81:94) stitches.
Continue without shaping in pattern until armholes measure
10(12:14:16:18)cm/4(4½:5½:6¼:7)ins from start of armhole shaping,
ending with a wrong side row.
shape shoulder
Cast off 11(15:19:23:27) stitches at the beginning of the next 2 rows.
Cast off centre 20(25:30:35:40) stitches.

front

With 3.75mm needles, cast on 50(59:72:85:98) stitches.
1st rib row: p2(4:2:4:2), [k3, p2]3(3:4:4:5) times, k0(0:2:3:4),
p0(0:2:2:2), k3(4:2:3:4), p1, k3(4:2:3:4), p0(0:2:2:2), k0(0:2:3:4),
p2(3:2:3:2), k0(0:2:3:4), p0(0:2:2:2), k3(4:2:3:4), p1, k3(4:2:3:4),
p0(0:2:2:2), k0(0:2:3:4), [p2, k3]3(3:4:4:5) times, p2(4:2:4:2).
2nd rib row: k2(4:2:4:2), [p3, k2]3(3:4:4:5) times, p0(0:2:3:4),
k0(0:2:2:2), p3(4:2:3:4), k1, p3(4:2:3:4), k0(0:2:2:2), p0(0:2:3:4),
k2(3:2:3:2), p0(0:2:3:4), k0(0:2:2:2), p3(4:2:3:4), k1, p3(4:2:3:4),
k0(0:2:2:2), p0(0:2:3:4), [k2, p3]3(3:4:4:5) times, k2(4:2:4:2).
These 2 rows form the rib pattern.
Repeat the last 2 rows 1(1:2:3:4) times more.

By Jane Ellison

Oxenber Tank Top

Increase row (right side): p2(4:2:4:2), [k3, p2]3(3:4:4:5) times, k1(1:1:2:3), m1, k2(2:4:4:4), m0(1:1:1:1), k0(1:1:2:3), p1, k1(1:1:2:3), m1, k2(2:4:4:4), m0(1:1:1:1), k0(1:1:2:3), p2(3:2:3:2), k1(1:1:2:3), m1, k2(2:4:4:4), m0(1:1:1:1), k0(1:1:2:3), p1, k1(1:1:2:3), m1, k2(2:4:4:4), m0(1:1:1:1), k0(1:1:2:3), [p2, k3]3(3:4:4:5) times, p2(4:2:4:2). 54(67:80:93:106) stitches
Change to 4mm needles.

Next row (wrong side): k2(4:2:4:2), [p3, k2] 3(3:4:4:5) times, p4(6:8:10:12), k1, p4(6:8:10:12), k2(3:2:3:2), p4(6:8:10:12), k1, p4(6:8:10:12), [k2, p3]3(3:4:4:5) times, k2(4:2:4:2).

1st row: p2(4:2:4:2), [k3, p2]3(3:4:4:5) times, C4(6:8:10:12)B, p1, C4(6:8:10:12)F, p2(3:2:3:2), C4(6:8:10:12)B, p1, C4(6:8:10:12)F, [p2, k3]3(3:4:4:5) times, p2(4:2:4:2).

2nd and every alternate row: k2(4:2:4:2), [p3, k2]3(3:4:4:5) times, p4(6:8:10:12), k1, p4(6:8:10:12), k2(3:2:3:2), p4(6:8:10:12), k1, p4(6:8:10:12), [k2, p3]3(3:4:4:5) times, k2(4:2:4:2).

3rd row: p2(4:2:4:2), [k3, p2]3(3:4:4:5) times, k4(6:8:10:12), p1, k4(6:8:10:12), p2(3:2:3:2), k4(6:8:10:12), p1, k4(6:8:10:12), [p2, k3]3(3:4:4:5) times, p2(4:2:4:2).
These 4 rows form the pattern.
Repeat the last 4 rows until front measures 14(16:20:24:28)cm/ 5½(6¼:7¾:9½:11)ins from cast on edge, ending with a wrong side row.

shape left armhole and neck
Cast off 3 stitches, pattern until there are 24(30:37:43:50) stitches, turn and leave remaining 27(34:40:47:53) stitches on a holder, pattern to end.

Decrease row (right side): k1, s1, k1, psso, pattern to last 12(16:20:24:28) stitches, p2togtbl, pattern to end. 22(28:35:41:48) stitches
Work 3 rows.
Repeat the last 4 rows twice more. 18(24:31:37:44) stitches

Neck decrease row (right side): pattern to last 12(16:20:24:28) stitches, p2togtbl, pattern to end. 17(23:30:36:43) stitches
Work one row.

Decrease one stitch at neck edge as set above until there are 11(15:19:23:27) stitches, ending with wrong side row.
Continue without shaping in pattern until armhole measures 10(12:14:16:18)cm/4(4½:5½:6¼:7)ins from start of armhole shaping, ending with a wrong side row.
Cast off.

shape right neck
With right side facing, rejoin yarn to remaining 27(34:40:47:53) stitches, cast off centre 0(1:0:1:0) stitches, pattern to end. 27(33:40:46:53) stitches
Cast off 3 stitches at the beginning of the next row. 24(30:37:43:50) stitches

Decrease row (right side): pattern 10(14:18:22:26) stitches, p2tog, pattern to last 3 stitches, k2tog, k1.
Work 3 rows.
Repeat the last 4 rows twice more. 18(24:31:37:44) stitches

Neck decrease row (right side): pattern 10(14:18:22:26) stitches, p2tog, pattern to end. 17(23:30:36:43) stitches
Work one row.

Decrease one stitch at neck edge as set above until there are 11(15:19:23:27) stitches, ending with wrong side row.
Continue without shaping in pattern until armhole measures 10(12:14:16:18)cm/4(4½:5½:6¼:7)ins from start of armhole shaping, ending with a wrong side row.
Cast off.

to make up

Join shoulder seams. Join side seams.

Wharfe Hat

Cable Hat

This is a fun cable hat which you can knit with or without the pom pom. The little cables make me think of the circle of life or little circles of joy!

MATERIALS

One 100g hank of dk weight yarn.
(this amount is based on dk weight
yarn with 225m per 100g)
Pair of 3.75mm knitting needles.
Pair of 4mm knitting needles.

to make

With 3.75mm needles, cast on 87(101:115) stitches.
1st rib row (right side): p3, k4, [p3, k4]to last 3 stitches, p3.
2nd rib row: k3, p4, [k3, p4]to last 3 stitches, k3.
These 2 rows form the rib pattern.
Repeat the last 2 rows once more.
Then the **1st rib row** once again.
Increase row (wrong side): k3, p4, [k1, m1, k2, p4]to last 3 stitches, k3. 98(114:130) stitches
Change to 4mm needles.
1st row (right side): p1, [T4B, T4F]to last stitch, p1.
2nd row: k1, p2, k4, [p4, k4]to last 3 stitches, p2, k1.
3rd row: p1, k2, p4, [k4, p4]to last 3 stitches, k2, p1.
4th row: as **2nd row**.
5th row: p1, [T4F, T4B]to last stitch, p1.
6th row: k3, p4, [k4, p4]to last 3 stitches, k3.
7th row: p3, k4, [p4, k4]to last 3 stitches, p3.
8th row: as **6th row**.
These 8 rows form the pattern.
Repeat the last 8 rows until hat measures approximately 15(15:18)cm/ 6(6:7)ins from cast on edge, ending with a **2nd row**.

TENSION

24 stitches and 24 rows to 10cm/4ins square
over pattern using 4mm needles.

TO FIT (SUGGESTED)

Newborn, Baby, Child.

shape crown

1st decrease row: k2tog, s1, k1, psso, p2,
[k2tog, k2, s1, k1, psso, p2]to last 4 stitches,
k2tog, s1, k1, psso. 72(84:96) stitches
Next row: p2, k2, [p4, k2]to last 2 stitches, p2.
2nd decrease row: k1, s1, k1, psso, k2tog, [k2, s1, k1, psso, k2tog]to last stitch, k1. 48(56:64) stitches
Next row: purl to end.
3rd decrease row: [k1, s1, k2tog, psso]to end. 24(28:32) stitches
Next row: purl to end.
4th decrease row: k1, [s1, k1, psso]to last stitch, k1. 13(15:17) stitches
5th decrease row: [p2tog]to last stitch, p1. 7(8:9) stitches
Break off yarn.
Thread through 7(8:9) stitches.
Pull securely and fasten off.

to make up

Sew side seam together.
Sew in ends neatly.
Make pom pom and secure to top of hat, if desired.

Rukin Cardigan
Traditional Cable Cardigan

MATERIALS

3(3:4:4:5) 100g hanks of aran weight yarn.
(this amount is based on aran weight
yarn with 166m per 100g)
Pair of 4.5mm knitting needles.
Pair of 5mm knitting needles.
5(6:6:7:7) buttons.

TENSION

28 stitches and 26 rows to 10cm/4ins square
over pattern using 5mm needles.

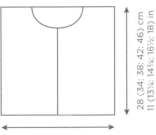

28 (34: 38: 42: 46) cm
11 (13¼: 14¾: 16½: 18) in

25 (27.5: 30: 32.5: 35) cm
9¾ (10¾: 11¾: 12¾: 13¾) in

18 (20: 24: 28: 36) cm
7 (7¾: 9½: 11: 14¼) in

15 (17: 19: 21: 23) cm
6 (6½: 7½: 8¼: 9) in

MEASUREMENTS

to fit (suggested age)	0-1	1-2	3-4	5-6	7-8	yrs
actual chest measurement	50	55	60	65	70	cm
	19½	21½	23½	25½	27½	ins
length	28	34	38	42	46	cm
	11	13¼	14¾	16½	18	ins
sleeve length	18	20	24	28	36	cm
	7	7¾	9½	11	14¼	ins

By Jane Ellison

Rukin Cardigan

This Cardigan is the sibling to the Crag Jumper however, this time the honeycomb cable wraps around the sides of the cardigan, giving a warm woolly hug to your little one when they're wearing it. My niece tells me that this is what is so special about wearing hand knits, she says it's like having a big hug all the time.

back

With 4.5mm needles, cast on 54(62:70:78:86) stitches.

1st rib row (right side): [p2, k2]4(5:6:7:8) times, p2, k4, [p2, k2]twice, p2, k4, p2, [k2, p2]to end.

2nd rib row: k2, p2]4(5:6:7:8) times, k2, p4, k2, [p2, k2]twice, p4, k2, [p2, k2]to end.

3rd rib row: [p2, k2]3(4:5:6:7) times, p2, C2F, p2, k4, p2, C2B, p2, C2F, p2, k4, p2, C2B, p2, [k2, p2]to end.

4th rib row: as **2nd rib row.**

5th rib row: as **3rd rib row.**

6th rib row: as **2nd rib row.**

Increase row (right side): p2, [k1, m1, k1, p1, m1(1:0:0:0), p1]2(3:4:5:6) times, m1(0:1:0:0), k1, m1(0:1:1:0), k1, p2, C2F, p2, k1, m1, k2, m1, k1, p2, C2B, p2, C2F, p2, k1, m1, k2, m1, k1, p2, C2B, p2, k1, m1(0:1:1:0), k1, m1(0:1:0:0), [p1, m1, p1, k1, m1(1:0:0:0), k1]2(3:4:5:6) times, p2.
70(78:86:94:102) stitches

Next row (wrong side): k2, p16(20:24:28:32), [k2, p2, k2, p6, k2, p2]twice, k2, p16(20:24:28:32), k2.

Change to 5mm needles.

1st row (right side): p2, [C4B, C4F]2(2:3:3:4) times, C0(4:0:4:0)B, p2, [C2F, p2, k2, C4F, p2, C2B, p2]twice, [C4B, C4F]2(2:3:3:4) times, C0(4:0:4:0)B, p2.

2nd and every alternate row: k2, p16(20:24:28:32), [k2, p2, k2, p6, k2, p2]twice, k2, p16(20:24:28:32), k2.

3rd row: p2, k16(20:24:28:32), p2, [C2F, p2, C4B, k2, p2, C2B, p2]twice, k16(20:24:28:32), p2.

5th row: p2, [C4F, C4B]2(2:3:3:4) times, C0(4:0:4:0)F, p2, [C2F, p2, k2, C4F, p2, C2B, p2]twice, [C4F, C4B]2(2:3:3:4) times, C0(4:0:4:0)F, p2.

7th row: as **3rd row**.

These 8 rows form the pattern.

Repeat the last 8 rows until back measures 28(34:38:42:46)cm/ 11(13¼:14¾:16½:18)ins from cast on edge, ending with a wrong side row.

shape shoulders

Cast off 21(24:27:30:33) stitches at the beginning of the next 2 rows.

Leave remaining 28(30:32:34:36) stitches on a holder.

left front

With 4.5mm needles, cast on 27(31:35:39:43) stitches.

1st rib row (right side): [p2, k2]to last 11 stitches, p2, k4, p2, k3.

2nd rib rows: p3, k2, p4, k2, [p2, k2]to end.

3rd rib row: p2, [k2, p2]to last 13 stitches, C2F, p2, k4, p2, C2B, k1.

4th rib row: as **2nd rib row.**

5th rib row: as **3rd rib row.**

6th rib row: as **2nd rib row.**

Increase row (right side): p2, [k1, m1, k1, p1, m1(1:0:0:0), p1]2(3:4:5:6) times, m1(0:1:0:0), k1, m1(0:1:1:0), k1, p2, C2F, p2, k1, m1, k2, m1, k1, p2, C2B, k1. 35(39:43:47:51) stitches

Next row: p3, k2, p6, k2, p2, k2, p16(20:24:28:32), k2.

Change to 5mm needles.

1st row (right side): p2, [C4B, C4F]2(2:3:3:4) times, C0(4:0:4:0)B, p2, C2F, p2, k2, C4F, p2, C2B, k1.

2nd and every alternate row: p3, k2, p6, k2, p2, k2, p16(20:24:28:32), k2.

3rd row: p2, k16(20:24:28:32), p2, C2F, p2, C4B, k2, p2, C2B, k1.

5th row: p2, [C4F, C4B]2(2:3:3:4) times, C0(4:0:4:0)F, p2, C2F, p2, k2, C4F, p2, C2B, k1.

7th row: as **3rd row.**

These 8 rows form the pattern.

Repeat the last 8 rows until left front measures 22(28:32:36:40)cm/ 8¾(11:12½:14¼:15¾)ins from cast on edge, ending with a **right side** row.

shape neck

Next row (wrong side): pattern 12(13:14:15:16) stitches, place these stitches on a holder, pattern to end. 23(26:29:32:35) stitches

Decrease row (right side): pattern to last 3 stitches, work2tog, work one stitch. 22(25:28:31:34) stitches

Work one row.

Decrease one stitch at neck edge as set above on the next row. 21(24:27:30:33) stitches

Continue in pattern until left front measures 28(34:38:42:46)cm/ 11(13¼:14¾:16½:18)ins from cast on edge, ending with a wrong side row.

Cast off.

By Jane Ellison

right front

With 4.5mm needles, cast on 27(31:35:39:43) stitches.
1st rib row (right side): k3, p2, k4, p2, [k2, p2]to end.
2nd rib rows: [k2, p2]to last 11 stitches, k2, p4, k2, p3.
3rd rib row: k1, C2F, p2, k4, p2, C2B, p2, [k2, p2]to end.
4th rib row: as **2nd rib row.**
5th rib row: as **3rd rib row.**
6th rib row: as **2nd rib row.**
Increase row (right side): k1, C2F, p2, k1, m1, k2, m1, k1, p2, C2B, p2, k1, m1(0:1:1:0), k1, m1(0:1:0:0), [p1, m1(1:0:0:0), p1, k1, m1, k1]2(3:4:5:6) times, p2. 35(39:43:47:51) stitches
Next row: k2, p16(20:24:28:32), k2, p2, k2, p6, k2, p3.
Change to 5mm needles.
1st row (right side): k1, C2F, p2, k2, C4F, p2, C2B, p2, [C4B, C4F]2(2:3:3:4) times, C0(4:0:4:0)B, p2.
2nd and every alternate row: k2, p16(20:24:28:32), k2, p2, k2, p6, k2, p3.
3rd row: k1, C2F, p2, C4B, k2, p2, C2B, p2, k16(20:24:28:32), p2.
5th row: k1, C2F, p2, k2, C4F, p2, C2B, p2, [C4F, C4B]2(2:3:3:4) times, C0(4:0:4:0)F, p2.
7th row: as **3rd row.**
These 8 rows form the pattern.
Work as given for left front, reversing neck shaping and working neck decreases as follows:
Decrease row (right side): p1, p2tog, pattern to end.

sleeves

With 4.5mm needles, cast on 34(38:42:46:50) stitches.
1st rib row: k2, [p2, k2]to end.
2nd rib row: p2, [k2, p2]to end.
These 2 rows form the pattern.
Repeat the last 2 rows once more.
Increase row (right side): [k2, p2]1(2:2:3:3) time(s), [k1, m1, k1, p2]6 times, k2, [p2, k2]1(1:2:2:3) time(s). 40(44:48:52:56) stitches
Next row (wrong side): p2, k2, p0(2:0:2:0), p32(32:40:40:48), p0(2:0:2:), p2, k2.
Change to 5mm needles.
1st row (right side): p4(6:4:6:4), [C4B, C4F]4(4:5:5:6) times, p4(6:4:6:4).
2nd and every alternate row: k4(6:4:6:4), p32(32:40:40:48), k4(6:4:6:4).
3rd row: p4(6:4:6:4), k32(32:40:40:48), p4(6:4:6:4).
5th row: p4(6:4:6:4), [C4F, C4B]4(4:5:5:6) times, p4(6:4:6:4).
7th row: as **3rd row.**
These 8 rows form the pattern.
Keeping pattern correct and taking increase stitches into reverse stocking stitch, increase one stitch at each end on next and every following 4th row until there are 56(60:64:68:72) stitches.
Continue without shaping in pattern until sleeve measures 18(20:24:28:36)cm/7(7¾:9½:11:14¼)ins from cast on edge, ending with a wrong side row.
Cast off.

buttonband left edging

Join shoulder seams. With right side facing and 4.5mm needles, pick up and knit 48(60:64:68:72) stitches down left front opening edge.
1st rib row (wrong side): p3, [k2, p2]to last stitch, p1.
2nd rib row: k3, [p2, k2]to last stitch, k1.
These 2 rows form the rib pattern.
Repeat the last 2 rows once more.
Cast off in rib pattern on wrong side.

buttonhole right edging

With right side facing and 4.5mm needles, pick up and knit 48(60:64:68:72) stitches up right front opening edge.
Work the **1st rib row** as given for **buttonband left edging.**
buttonhole row (right side): k1, *k2tog, yon, p2, [k2, p2]twice, repeat from * to last 11(11:15:7:11) stitches, k2tog, yon, [p2, k2]2(2:3:1:2) time(s), k1 .
Work 2 rows in rib pattern.
Cast off in rib pattern on wrong side.

neck edging

With right side facing and 4.5mm needles, pick up and knit 4 stitches from buttonhole right edging, work across the 12(13:14:15:16) stitches from holder at right front as follows: k1, C2F, p2, s1, k1, psso, k2, k2tog, p1(2:2:2:2), C0(0:0:2:2)B, k0(0:1:0:1), to make 10(11:12:13:14) stitches, pick up and knit 10(12:10:12:10) stitches up right front neck, work across the 28(30:32:34:36) stitches from holder at centre back as follows: k1(0:0:0:1), p0(0:1:2:2), C0(2:2:2:2)F, p2, s1, k1, psso, k2, k2tog, p2, C2B, p2, C2F, p2, s1, k1, psso, k2, k2tog, p2, C0(2:2:2:2)B, p0(0:1:2:2), k1(0:0:0:1), to make 24(26:28:30:32) stitches, pick up and knit 10(12:10:12:10) stitches down left front neck, work across the 12(13:14:15:16) stitches from holder at left front as follows: k0(0:1:0:1), C0(0:0:2:2)B, p1(2:2:2:2), s1, k1, psso, k2, k2tog, p2, C2F, k1, to make 10(11:12:13:14) stitches, pick up and knit 4 stitches from buttonband left edging. 72(80:80:88:88) stitches
1st row (wrong side): p3, k2, p2, k2, p4, k2, [p2, k2]3(4:4:5:5) times, p4, k2, [p2, k2]twice, p4, k2, [p2, k2]3(4:4:5:5) times, p4, k2, p2, k2, p3.
buttonhole row (right side): k1, k2tog, yon, p2, C2F, p2, k4, p2, [k2, p2]2(3:3:4:4) times, C2F, p2, k4, p2, C2B, p2, C2F, p2, k4, p2, C2B, [p2, k2]2(3:3:4:4) times, p2, k4, p2, C2B, p2, k3.
3rd row: as **1st row.**
4th row: k3, p2, C2F, p2, k4, p2, [k2, p2]2(3:3:4:4) times, C2F, p2, k4, p2, C2B, p2, C2F, p2, k4, p2, C2B, [p2, k2](3:3:4:4) times, p2, k4, p2, C2B, p2, k3.
Cast off in rib pattern on wrong side row.

to make up

Sew on sleeves, placing centre of sleeves to shoulder seams. Join side and sleeve seams. Position and sew buttons into place.

Basic Tips

With the correct yarn and needles, knitting can be successful and satisfying. You are creating your own garment which, with practice and experience, you can make to your requirements; your very own bespoke garment for your little loved one! The ultimate gift of love and joy.

Tension (gauge)

This is a simple and easy step of knitting a tension square before every pattern.

The importance of a tension square can mean the difference between a garment that is twice the size it should be and one that is the correct size.

Every pattern has its own unique tension and this is measured over a 10cm/4ins square. It is the number of stitches and rows in this square.

To make a tension square, first cast on the amount of stitches stated in the tension part of the pattern, THEN cast on an extra 10 stitches, or the nearest amount to this to fit into the pattern repeat. Work in the pattern, in this example it is stocking stitch, until the square measures 12cm/4¾ins from cast on edge.

Don't cast off but instead break off the yarn and thread through the stitches, taking them off the needle.

To count the stitches in your tension square, lay it down flat. On stocking stitch, a stitch makes a 'V' shape, place a pin by the side of one 'V' and measure 10cm/4ins horizontally with a tape measure and mark this with a pin. Count the stitches between the pins.

With the rows, the same 'V' is now a row and by placing your tape measure and pins vertically you can count the rows.

If you have the stated amount of stitches and rows between the pins you have the correct tension and can commence your chosen pattern.

If you have too many stitches, your tension is tight and your garment will be smaller than stated. Change to a larger needle.

If there are too few stitches, your tension is loose and your garment will be bigger than stated. Change to a smaller needle.

Sizing Information

In each pattern there are measurements, which include 'To fit (suggested age)' ages in years and 'Actual Chest Measurement' sizes. There are also diagrams of the garment. These show the garment's width at the underarm and total body length.

The ages are suggested because, as we all know, children grow and develop at the rate that is perfect for them. I don't like standardising sizes, for either adults or children because we are the perfect size for us and shouldn't be compared to anyone else. Having said that, we have to start from somewhere so I use the sizes as just that – a starting point – then work from there, double checking that the actual chest measurement will work for the look I'm after.

I recommend that the best way to get the right size is to do the following:

Once you have chosen the garment you wish to knit, find a similar garment that fits the child you are knitting for. Lay the existing garment out flat and measure across the chest (about 2cm/1in under the armholes). Once you have this figure, compare it to the width measurements on the diagrams and chose the knitted garment size that is nearest to this figure.

If you want to lengthen or shorten the garment, the best place to do this is in the instructions before the 'Shape Armholes' instruction, if the pattern has this instruction. Otherwise it is just the total length. Remember to work the same length on the back and front or fronts.

The same principle applies to the sleeves. Just like adults, children all have different length arms. If you are not sure, always make it slightly too long because you can always roll up the cuff. Once you have knitted the back and front, pin or sew the shoulders together. Pin the side seams and put the garment shell on the child. Measure from the seam under the arm to the desired length.

To lengthen or shorten the sleeve, find the instruction in the pattern that states, for example: 'Continue without shaping in garter stitch until sleeve measures 20(22:24:26:28)cm/7¾(8¾:9½:10¼:11)ins from cast on edge, ending with a wrong side row.'

Change this measurement by your different amount to make your garment truly unique, just like the little one you are knitting for.

Finishing Techniques

When knitting a garment, what's really important is that making that first stitch, then another, then another leads to your mind calming down, your shoulders falling and you starting to relax.

It's all about focusing on one stitch at a time, then, before you know it, you've knitted a back or a front, or some sleeves. The magic of creating a garment in this way is what makes knitting so enjoyable.

I love sewing up garments; I sewed up and picked up stitches on every single one of the garments for this book. I especially love picking up stitches! Once I have knitted the pieces, I make them into piles and save them up for a lovely sewing up session

I do understand though, that this part of the garment journey may not be quite so enjoyable for new knitters or even experienced knitters who haven't been shown the best ways to sew up a garment.

I also understand that it's not a task to be undertaken when tired because, unlike knitting which rests the mind, sewing up does need a bit of concentration.

So I have put together a few pieces of advice to help you enjoy sewing up too. It is a bit tricky to explain something so tactile through the written word so I've made a series of videos of the following techniques to make it easier to follow.

You can find all my videos on my YouTube channel https://www.youtube.com/user/purlandjane

To make sewing up fun, we can start with just two simple techniques: mattress stitch and grafting the shoulders. Both use specialised stitches and mean you sew up the garment as a knitted piece and do not treat it like a piece of cloth.

Grafting the shoulders or the 3 needle cast off.

This involves ignoring an instruction in the pattern. Instead of casting off the stitches for the shoulders, leave these on a holder. When you have completed the back and front (or fronts), the pattern will then instruct you to join shoulder seams.

This is the simple way to do this:

You will need 3 knitting needles (take a long deep breath, this is easier than it sounds when written down!). Place the stitches on the holder for one back shoulder onto a needle, then place the stitches on the holder for a front shoulder onto another needle. Place the right sides together and the two knitting needles together in your left hand facing the same direction, as if both needles were one. Take the third knitting needle in your right hand and start to cast off, treating the two needles as if they were one. This means that you insert your needle into the first stitch on the first needle and first stitch on the second needle, knit both of the stitches. Do this with the second stitch, and then slip the first stitch on the right hand needle over the second stitch. Repeat this until all stitches have been worked.

Mattress stitch

To sew the garment's sides together I suggest a magical stitch that makes sewing up enjoyable. I have written the patterns so the stitch repeats work beautifully with this sewing up technique. It is called the mattress stitch and it is so magical you can use a different coloured thread if you want to and it will not show on the right side!

I think it is called the mattress stitch because you are always working the front of the garment and your needle never goes behind the garment, almost like sewing the edges of a mattress together and if you put that needle into the mattress it will be lost! I've been told that this is also the stitch that surgeons use to sew up scars (though I've also been told they now staple them together instead!).

Here are the instructions for the mattress stitch:

With the right sides facing, work one stitch in from the edge. When looking at stocking stitch, there are 'V' shapes and, when the knitting is slightly pulled, there are bars in between these Vs. These are the bars that are used in mattress stitch as the needle is woven in and out of them. Starting at one side, and using a darning needle, insert the needle under the first two bars and up, then insert the needle at the same point on the other side, going under and behind the first two bars. Go to the other side inserting the needle into the same place where the thread came. After you have completed this for a few cms/ins, pull the yarn and watch the two sides come together with an invisible seam! Remember to weave backwards and forwards between the two sides, and do not sew into the sides at all.

Abbreviations

Knitting has a language of its own. Instructions for making a knitted item use abbreviated terms, here are the ones I've used in this book:

cm	centimetres.
C2B	miss the first stitch by passing in front of it and knitting into the front of the second stitch, then knit the first stitch, slip both stitches off the needle.
C2F	miss the first stitch by passing behind it and knitting into the back of the second stitch, then knit the first stitch, slip both stitches off the needle.
C4B	slip next 2 stitches onto cable needle and leave at back of work, k2, then k2 from cable needle.
C4F	slip next 2 stitches onto cable needle and leave at front of work, k2, then k2 from cable needle.
C6B	slip next 3 stitches onto cable needle and leave at back of work, k3, then k3 from cable needle.
C6F	slip next 3 stitches onto cable needle and leave at front of work, k3, then k3 from cable needle.
C8B	slip next 4 stitches onto cable needle and leave at back of work, k4, then k4 from cable needle.
C8F	slip next 4 stitches onto cable needle and leave at front of work, k4, then k4 from cable needle.
C10B	slip next 5 stitches onto cable needle and leave at back of work, k5, then k5 from cable needle.
C10F	slip next 5 stitches onto cable needle and leave at front of work, k5, then k5 from cable needle.
C12F	slip next 6 stitches onto cable needle and leave at front of work, k6, then k6 from cable needle.
C12B	slip next 6 stitches onto cable needle and leave at back of work, k6, then k6 from cable needle.
CDF	slip next 2 stitches onto cable needle and leave at front of work, k2tog, k2tog from cable needle.
k	knit.
inc 1	increase one stitch by knitting into the back and front of the stitch.
in(s)	inch(es).
garter stitch	knit every row.
s1	slip one stitch.
stocking stitch	knit one row, purl one row.
T4B	slip next 2 stitches onto cable needle, leave at back of work, k2, then p2 from cable needle.
T4F	slip next 2 stitches onto cable needle, leave at front of work, p2, then k2 from cable needle.
tbl	through back of loop.
tog	together.
p	purl.
psso	pass slip stitch over.
m1	make one stitch by picking up the loop lying between the stitch just worked and the next stitch and working into the back of the loop.
yon	yarn over needle.
ybk	yarn back between the two needles.
yfwd	yarn forward between the two needles.

General Pattern Information

(round brackets) In the pattern the instructions are given for the smallest size, with larger sizes in (round) brackets.

Where only one figure or instruction is given this applies to all sizes.

[square brackets] working all directions inside [square] brackets the number of times stated or until the correct number of stitches remain.

USA Glossary

cast off	bind off
tension	gauge
stocking stitch	stockinette stitch